FACING THE GIANTS IN YOUR LIFE

D1292059

Dr. David Jeremiah

with Dr. David Jeremiah

CONTENTS

ABOUT
DR. DAVID JEREMIAH
AND TURNING POINT

D r. David Jeremiah is the founder of Turning Point, a ministry committed to providing Christians with sound Bible teaching relevant to today's changing times through radio broadcasts, audiocassette series, and books. Dr. Jeremiah's "common-sense" teaching on topics such as family, stress, the New Age, angels, and biblical prophecy forms the foundation of Turning Point.

Dr. Jeremiah is the senior pastor of Shadow Mountain Community Church in El Cajon near San Diego, California, where he also serves as chancellor of Christian Heritage College. He and his wife, Donna, have four children and three grandchildren.

In 1982, Dr. Jeremiah brought the same solid teaching to San Diego television that he shares weekly with his congregation. Shortly thereafter, Turning Point expanded its ministry to radio and now national television. Dr. Jeremiah's inspiring messages are currently broadcast weekly from more than 1000 national and international radio outlets.

Because Dr. Jeremiah desires to know his listening audience, he travels nationwide holding "A Night of Encouragement" radio rallies that touch the hearts and lives of many. According to Dr. Jeremiah, "At some point in time, everyone reaches a turning point, and for every person that moment is unique, an experience to hold onto forever. There's so much changing in today's world that sometimes it's difficult to choose the right path. Turning Point offers people an understanding of God's Word, as well as the opportunity to make a difference in their lives."

Dr. Jeremiah has authored numerous books, including *Escape the Coming Night* (Revelation), *The Handwriting on the Wall* (Daniel), *Turning Toward Joy* (Philippians), *Invasion of Other Gods* (New Age), *Overcoming Loneliness*, *What the Bible Says About Angels*, *The Power of Encouragement*, *Prayer—The Great Adventure*, *God in You* (Holy Spirit), *Gifts from God* (Parenting), *Jesus' Final Warning*, and *A Bend in the Road*.

When possible, the study guide should be used with the
esponding tape series. You may wish to assign the study guide
omework prior to the meeting of the group and then use the
eting time to listen to the tape and discuss the lesson.

R CONTINUING STUDY

A complete catalog of Dr. Jeremiah's materials for personal
d group study is available through Turning Point. To obtain
atalog, additional study guides, or more information about
rning Point, call 1-800-947-1993 or write to: Turning Point,
). Box 3838, San Diego, CA 92163.

Dr. Jeremiah's *Turning Point* radio broadcast is currently heard
more than 1000 national and international radio outlets. Contact
rning Point for radio and television program times and stations in
ur area.

ABOUT THIS STUDY GUIDE

T he purpose of this Turning Point study guide is ¹
Dr. David Jeremiah's dynamic, in-depth teaching
the Giants in Your Life and to aid the reader in app
biblical truth to his or her daily life. This study guide is d
be used in conjunction with Dr. Jeremiah's *Facing the Gian*
Life audiocassette series, but it may be used by itself for pe
group Bible study.

STRUCTURE OF THE LESSONS

Each lesson is based on one of the tapes in the *Facing th*
Your Life audiocassette series and focuses on specific passag
Bible. Each lesson is composed of the following elements:

- *Outline*

The outline at the beginning of the lesson gives a clear,
concise picture of the passage being studied and provides a h
framework for readers as they listen to Dr. Jeremiah's teaching

- *Overview*

The overview summarizes Dr. Jeremiah's teaching on the p
being studied in the lesson. Readers should refer to the biblical
passages in their own Bibles as they study the overview.

- *Application*

This section contains a variety of questions designed to help
readers dig deeper into the lesson and the Scriptures and to apply
the lesson to their daily lives. For Bible study groups or Sunday
school classes, these questions will provide a springboard for group
discussion and interaction.

- *Did You Know?*

This section presents a fascinating fact, historical note, or insight
that adds a point of interest to the preceding lesson.

USING THIS GUIDE FOR GROUP STUDY

The lessons in this study guide are suitable for Sunday school
classes, small-group studies, elective Bible studies, or home Bible
study groups. Each person in the group should have his or her own
study guide.

ABOUT THIS
STUDY GUIDE

The purpose of this Turning Point study guide is to reinforce Dr. David Jeremiah's dynamic, in-depth teaching on *Facing the Giants in Your Life* and to aid the reader in applying biblical truth to his or her daily life. This study guide is designed to be used in conjunction with Dr. Jeremiah's *Facing the Giants in Your Life* audiocassette series, but it may be used by itself for personal or group Bible study.

STRUCTURE OF THE LESSONS

Each lesson is based on one of the tapes in the *Facing the Giants in Your Life* audiocassette series and focuses on specific passages in the Bible. Each lesson is composed of the following elements:

- *Outline*

The outline at the beginning of the lesson gives a clear, concise picture of the passage being studied and provides a helpful framework for readers as they listen to Dr. Jeremiah's teaching.

- *Overview*

The overview summarizes Dr. Jeremiah's teaching on the passage being studied in the lesson. Readers should refer to the biblical passages in their own Bibles as they study the overview.

- *Application*

This section contains a variety of questions designed to help readers dig deeper into the lesson and the Scriptures and to apply the lesson to their daily lives. For Bible study groups or Sunday school classes, these questions will provide a springboard for group discussion and interaction.

- *Did You Know?*

This section presents a fascinating fact, historical note, or insight that adds a point of interest to the preceding lesson.

USING THIS GUIDE FOR GROUP STUDY

The lessons in this study guide are suitable for Sunday school classes, small-group studies, elective Bible studies, or home Bible study groups. Each person in the group should have his or her own study guide.

When possible, the study guide should be used with the corresponding tape series. You may wish to assign the study guide as homework prior to the meeting of the group and then use the meeting time to listen to the tape and discuss the lesson.

FOR CONTINUING STUDY

A complete catalog of Dr. Jeremiah's materials for personal and group study is available through Turning Point. To obtain a catalog, additional study guides, or more information about Turning Point, call 1-800-947-1993 or write to: Turning Point, P.O. Box 3838, San Diego, CA 92163.

Dr. Jeremiah's *Turning Point* radio broadcast is currently heard on more than 1000 national and international radio outlets. Contact Turning Point for radio and television program times and stations in your area.

FACING THE GIANTS IN YOUR LIFE

INTRODUCTION

Sometimes we think how grateful we are not to live in the days of the Old Testament. Think about it—no airline travel, no computers, no television, no thirty-one flavors of ice cream. If we wanted to, we could make a list longer than an eight-year-old's Christmas list of all the reasons we're glad we weren't born in the days of the "-ites" (the Canaanites, the Perizzites, the Amalekites, and all the rest).

We're not to be faulted for our preference for modern times; things are better and easier in many ways than they were then. But for all our wisdom in preferring now to then, there is one big reason that most people fail to include on their list: There were giants in the land. That's right—real, live giants. Huge humans. Moving mountains. Shade-makers on legs. Given that we live in the age of Hollywood when it's getting hard to separate fact from fancy, we sometimes can be cynical about the record of that which was common thousands of years ago. But the Bible literally says there were giants that made life rough for God's people.

The Old Testament giants are first mentioned in Genesis 6:2. Some modern translations of the Bible refer to them by their Hebrew name, the Nephilim. Their descendants were still roaming around Canaan when Israel peeked over the border to inspect their promised land. With knees knocking, the spies Moses sent into the land returned to report that the descendants of Anak (sounds like a giant, doesn't it? Anak means "long-necked" in Hebrew) were in the land. The spies said they were like grasshoppers compared to the giants (Numbers 13:33). The last of a race of giants called the Rephaim was Og, the king of Bashan. His bed was—are you ready for this?—thirteen and a half feet long and six feet wide! (Deuteronomy 3:11). And who can forget old Goliath whose nine-foot frame struck fear into the entire army of Saul?

To put it bluntly, the Israelites were terrorized by the giants in the land. We probably would have been as well. But ask yourself this: How many of the Nephilim and Rephaim have you seen walking around lately? That's right—those giants are all dead and gone. But before you put your slingshot and stones away, I have something else to tell you. There's a whole new breed of giants alive and well in our day.

Unfortunately, you can't see these giants. In fact, they're sort of like the wind: You only know they're around when things start to shake. Because they sneak in on cat's paws, these giants can be walking right beside you before you even know it. What kind of giants am I talking about? They're the kind that can convince you you're a trespasser in the spiritual land God has promised you. They're the kind that can make you feel like God isn't going to keep His promises to you. And they're the kind that can make you wish you'd stayed in Egypt and never accepted God's offer of deliverance and salvation.

In this series of studies you'll come face to face with the spiritual giants that try to terrorize Christians all over the world—giants like fear, discouragement, loneliness, worry, guilt, temptation, anger, resentment, doubt, procrastination, failure, and jealousy. Have you met any of these giants? Do one or more of them have you in a spiritual headlock right now?

In these lessons you'll identify these invisible stranglers and learn how to break their hold on you. The only true spiritual giant, Jesus Christ, has gone ahead of us and defeated them all which is the real reason this is the best time to be alive!

FACING THE GIANT OF FEAR

Deuteronomy 1:19-40

---

*In this lesson we discover the devastating impact of fear—
and how to overcome it.*

OUTLINE

Fear is a God-given reaction which can protect us from harm. But
sometimes we are fearful when we shouldn't be. Understanding the
debilitating effects of inappropriate fear will go a long way toward
overcoming it—with God's help.

    I. **Fear Disregards God's Plan**

   II. **Fear Distorts God's Purposes**

  III. **Fear Discourages God's People**

  IV. **Fear Disbelieves God's Promises**

   V. **Fear Disobeys God's Principles**

  VI. **Fear Demands a Biblical Response**
      A. Confront Your Fear Honestly
      B. Confess Your Fear as Sin
      C. Claim God's Promises of Protection
      D. Cultivate a Closer Relationship with God
      E. Commit Your Life to Jesus Christ

OVERVIEW

This series of studies is not about the kinds of giants we read about in the Old Testament—giants like Goliath who stood more than nine feet tall. Instead, we're going to talk about another breed of giants which can be every bit as threatening to our well being: spiritual giants that invade our lives and seek to destroy the work of God in us.

The first of these giants we will study is the giant of fear. Many people have phobias—those irrational roadblocks that keep us from doing things we want to do. Some people are afraid of heights, some of open spaces, some of airplanes. There are more than one hundred different phobias, and about ten percent of the population suffers from one or more of them. But those phobias are not what we'll be studying in this series.

We will look at the spirit of fear that can take over your life and dominate you in a way God never intended. Fear is not always a bad thing. God uses fear to protect us—to keep us from doing things which might hurt us. But when fear becomes a permanent condition it can immobilize you and bring your entire life to a standstill.

Everyone experiences fear at different times. I experience fear at times when I have to stand and speak in front of a large crowd. Every parent has experienced fear when his or her children have been injured or thrust into new situations for which they are not prepared. And some of us have experienced fear when we are told that we have a serious disease. Ideally, those fears come and go; they don't dominate our lives. It's when fear takes over that we know there is a giant that needs to be conquered.

We see fear in understandable circumstances in Scripture. When the disciples were on the Sea of Galilee during a fierce storm, they were afraid. When the Israelites were accosted by the Philistine giant, Goliath, they were afraid. But the Old Testament story which best illustrates how to deal with fear is the story of the twelve spies who left Kadesh Barnea to spy out the Promised Land of Canaan. That story is told initially in Numbers 13-14, but it is repeated in a condensed version in Deuteronomy 1:19-40.

To set the stage, Israel has been freed from slavery in Egypt and is approaching the Promised Land under Moses' leadership. Before taking the whole nation in, Moses sends twelve men into the land to check it out—to see how formidable the inhabitants were, how well the cities were fortified, and how fertile the land was. When we see the response of some of the spies upon their return, we learn that fear has not changed in several thousand years.

FEAR DISREGARDS GOD'S PLAN

Verses 19-21 of chapter one clearly indicate that it was God's plan for the Israelites to go up and possess the land of Canaan. And verse 21 clearly reveals what would stand in their way to keep them from fulfilling God's plan—fear and discouragement. And that is exactly what controlled the people after hearing a negative report from ten of the spies.

Fear took hold of their lives, and they couldn't believe that God had actually brought them to the place of their inheritance and their blessing. Fear will keep you from experiencing God's plan in your life. We have an inheritance today just as the Israelites did in their day. Our inheritance is just as much the plan of God as was theirs. And we have just as clear a warning from the apostle Paul as Israel had from Moses—a warning about fear: "God has not given us a spirit of fear, but of power and of love and of a sound mind" (II Timothy 1:7). God has not created us to be creatures dominated by fear. He has given us the principle of faith upon which to live. If we choose to live in fear we are disregarding God's plan for our life.

The same principle is given by Paul in the book of Romans: "For you did not receive the spirit of bondage again to fear, but you received the spirit of adoption by whom we cry out, 'Abba, Father'" (Romans 8:15). God's plan for us, His desire for us, is that we live above fear, that we walk in the power of His love.

FEAR DISTORTS GOD'S PURPOSES

When fear dominates our life everything gets out of perspective; everything gets distorted. Ten of the twelve spies who returned to Kadesh Barnea brought back a totally distorted picture of what the Promised Land was really like. Their skewed report is found in verses 27-28. They came back and reported that the Promised Land was filled with Anakim, or giants. There were giants in the land of Canaan in those days (remember Goliath?), but not every person in Canaan was a giant. Their fear caused them to see one thing and report another. They saw great cities which were well fortified and concluded that they would never be able to take them. In fact, their fear so totally distorted their thinking that they concluded the only reason God had led them to Canaan was to destroy them!

You may think, "That is the most irrational thought you could ever have of God!" But when fear begins to control your life, you don't think correctly; rationality goes out the window. If you choose to let fear control your thinking, you will have a distorted view of the situation you are in and life in general. Everything will be totally out of perspective. You will think God has brought you into a terrible situation just to do you harm.

FEAR DISCOURAGES GOD'S PEOPLE

Not only does fear disregard God's plan and distort God's purposes, but it also discourages God's people. The kind of fear that controls is highly contagious—a communicable sin. Think of the situation in Israel at Kadesh Barnea. Ten men out of twelve came back from Canaan controlled by fear, and those ten men determined the destiny of the rest of the entire nation for the next forty years. Their words of fear so infected the rest of the people that the entire nation became fearful of going into the land God had promised. The fearful words of ten people turned the fortunes of an entire nation.

Somebody said that when the spies came back from the land of Canaan, they not only talked about the giants they saw, they brought one of the giants back with them—the giant of fear. And that giant walked into Israel's camp and destroyed everything that was in the heart of the whole nation. Fear like this is akin to someone yelling, "Fire!" in the midst of a crowded theatre. Without any knowledge of the facts, panic sets in and causes a stampede among hundreds of people. The entire landscape changes when one or more people are consumed by fear.

FEAR DISBELIEVES GOD'S PROMISES

You would think that when Israel stood on the threshold of the Promised Land and faced a new set of challenges they would have trusted God to see them through. Wasn't He the God who worked mighty miracles for them in Egypt? Moses outlined in verses 29-33 what God had done for Israel in the past and how, on the basis of His past promise-keeping, He would then keep His promises to deliver Israel into the land of milk and honey. But instead, fear caused Israel to disbelieve the promises of God.

Think of all the things God had done for them: The plagues, the parting of the Red Sea, the giving of the Law, the provision of water and food in the wilderness, defeating their enemies on the way, guiding them by a pillar of fire and a cloud. God carried Israel through the wilderness as a father carries a child. Shouldn't Israel, on the basis of all those demonstrations of God's power, have trusted Him one more time? I have found in my own walk with the Lord that each new test must be approached with new faith. We cannot live on yesterday's faith. Many Christians don't realize that they can trust God ten times in a row and then disbelieve Him the eleventh time if they allow fear to set in. Yielding to fear will lead to disbelieving the promises of God.

FEAR DISOBEYS GOD'S PRINCIPLES

When we don't believe, we usually don't obey. Verse 26 documents that Israel rebelled against the command of the Lord. This may sound a bit harsh, but I believe it to be true: Fear is disobeying God. Many, many times in the Bible we are told, "Fear not," or "Do not be afraid." Now, if we are told by God not to fear, and we choose to live in fear, what are we doing? We are disobeying God.

Because the people did not obey God, they did not go up into the land and receive from God what He had promised to give them. The entire generation of those adults who succumbed to the fear of the ten spies were kept from going up and receiving their inheritance in the land. That generation spent the next forty years wandering in the wilderness, slowly dying off, until their children's generation was of adult age. The only two people allowed to go into the land from the disobedient generation were Joshua and Caleb, the two spies who wanted the people to trust God for victory in the Promised Land.

When fear grips our lives it ultimately destroys everything God wants to do in and through us. I have known people to whom God has given a vision, a direction for life and ministry, but who failed to follow through with God because of fear. As a result, their lives became rambling, meaningless journeys instead of focused, purposeful missions. Fear can steal the very thing God wants to give us.

What do we do when fear is knocking on the door of our heart? How do we keep it from taking control? Five principles will protect you from being controlled by fear.

FEAR DEMANDS A BIBLICAL RESPONSE
Confront Your Fear Honestly

Fear doesn't just decide to act nice and leave you alone. You have to confront it to get rid of it. You must discover what it is that is giving fear an invitation to take up residence in your life and face it honestly. If you don't know what it is, ask God in prayer. Get counsel from a trusted friend or pastor. You can't get rid of what you can't identify.

Moody Monthly magazine (Sep/Oct, 1996) had a fascinating story about a Canadian family who was growing fearful about the likelihood of another world war. They wanted to move to a location in the world where peace would be assured. So they moved to the British-controlled Falkland Islands off the cost of Argentina in March, 1982. Five days later, the Argentine army invaded the Falkland Islands, and they found themselves in the middle of a war. That's how fear is. It will follow you wherever you go unless you confront it.

Confess Your Fear as Sin

I have touched on this already—if God says "Fear not," and we fear, we are disobeying God. And disobeying God is sin. You may think it is impossible to be able to command your feelings, to tell your feelings to "Fear not." You may not be able to command your feelings, but you can command your will to obey the voice of the Lord and fill your life with His truth. Psalm 34:4 says, "I sought the Lord, and He heard me, and delivered me from all my fears." Where our will goes, our feelings follow. If we seek the Lord, obey the Lord, dwell in the Lord, meditate on the Lord's word, we will find our feelings—including our feelings of fear—following closely behind. Too many people try to get rid of fear without recognizing it, and confessing it, as sin. What God has forgiven and removed will not have dominion over you.

Claim God's Promises of Protection

If I found myself overcome by fear, here is what I would do. I would take a stack of index cards and fill them with the verses from the Application section of this lesson (plus as many other verses on fear as I could locate). Put one verse on each card; then put the cards in places where you will see them all day long: on your car visor or dashboard, on the bathroom mirror, on the kitchen counter, on your desk at work, in your purse or wallet, in a coat pocket. Everywhere you go, take the Word of God with you to remind you of the truth about fear.

Wherever you are, when the spirit of fear begins to intimidate you, you will have the truth of God near at hand. Instead of allowing your mind to be filled with fearful lies, fill it with the Word of God. Tell the enemy when he begins whispering to you about fear, "Forget it. I have a word from God that says, 'Fear not!'"

Cultivate a Closer Relationship with God

Before dismissing this as elementary, think carefully with me. What was it about the two of the twelve spies who weren't fearful, the two who believed God would help them take the land? We get a clear picture of them from three passages of Scripture: Deuteronomy 1:36; Numbers 14:24; 32:12. To summarize, all three of these passages say that Joshua and Caleb "wholly followed the Lord." This was the difference between the two who were courageous and the ten who were fearful. They had a relationship with God that was the dominant force in their lives. As a result, there was no room for fear. When they saw giants and walled cities, they said, "Our God can handle this. What's to fear?" Where the others saw obstacles, Joshua and Caleb saw God.

God's perfect love casts out fear (I John 4:18). Just as a parent showers a fearful child with love and protection when he or she is frightened, so God enfolds us in His loving arms and casts out fear.

Commit Your Life to Jesus Christ

The greatest fear anyone could have is the fear of death (Hebrews 2:14-15). It only stands to reason that if the greatest fear is conquered, all lesser fears could be conquered as well. There is only one sure way to conquer the fear of death, and that is by accepting the gift of eternal life offered by Jesus Christ. If you are a Christian, certain of your eternal life, you have already conquered the greatest fear. No other fear should concern you. If you are not a Christian, and live not only in fear of death but of other things as well, I invite you to begin this series of lessons by accepting God's gift of love for you, Jesus Christ. Remember: His perfect love casts out all fear.

APPLICATION

1. Read Deuteronomy 31:1-8.
    a. What did Moses tell the Israelites God would do for them when they crossed over the Jordan River into the Promised Land? (verses 3-5)

    b. What were the four responsibilities given to the Israelites? (verse 6)

    c. Why would the Israelites be able, in good faith, to be courageous? (verse 6)

    d. What is the connection between the resources one has and one's ability to be courageous?

    e. Therefore, if a Christian has God on his side, how courageous should he be?

    f. What instruction did Moses give to Joshua? (verse 7)

    g. What is the connection between a leader's level of courage and the level of courage of those he leads?

    h. If Joshua had been fearful and failed to obey God, what would the Israelites likely have done?

    i. What promises about God's presence do you find in verse 8?

    j. Hebrews 13:5 is an oft-quoted verse in the New Testament. Read it, then record how it helps your understanding of this New Testament promise, knowing the situation in which it was originally spoken (verse 8).

2. Read 1 Chronicles 28:20.
   a. What word does David use that would indicate whether Solomon was really "strong and of good courage?"

   b. In overcoming fear, there are two parts: God's part and our part. How would you describe God's part?

   c. How would you describe our part?

   c. How will a person who is afraid of heights know if he has overcome that fear?

   d. Describe something (past or present) you have been postponing doing because of fear?

   e. What is God's part in the situation?

   f. What is your part?

   g. How will you know when you have conquered that fear?

3. Read Psalm 27:1, 13-14.
   a. In what three ways is the Lord described in verse 1?

   b. How do each of these three descriptions of God help to dispel fear in the life of the believer?

   c. What will happen unless we exercise faith in God's strength and attributes? (verse 13)

   d. What do we sometimes have to do in order to gain strength from the Lord? (verse 14)

e. What does it mean to "wait on the Lord"? (See the fourth of the five Biblical responses to fear in this lesson.)

4. Read Isaiah 41:8-10.
   a. What parallels do you find in God's description of Israel in verse 8 and Paul's description of himself in Romans 1:1?

   b. Fill in the reasons God says what He says to those He calls (verse 10).

   • Fear not, for . . .

   • Be not dismayed, for . . .

   c. What three things does God promise to do for those facing fear-inducing circumstances:
   (1)

   (2)

   (3)

DID YOU KNOW?

Fear can be a good thing. *The American Heritage Dictionary* says fear is "a feeling of agitation and anxiety caused by the presence or imminence of danger." If we are planning on wading through a snake infested swamp, we have every reason to entertain a healthy sense of fear. But if our goal is to wade across the shallow end of a swimming pool, we shouldn't be afraid. What makes fear legitimate in one circumstance but not the other? It's the circumstance itself. If we are in danger, fear might save our life. If we are not in danger, then fear is a false obstacle which should be overcome. Common sense and wisdom from God can show the difference. Fear can be a life saver or a life taker.

FACING THE GIANT OF DISCOURAGEMENT

Nehemiah 4

In this lesson we learn what can bring on discouragement and how to defend ourselves against it.

OUTLINE

Martin Luther said, "You can't keep the birds from flying overhead but you can keep them from nesting in your hair." The giant of discouragement is always lurking. Knowing how he arrives and how to send him packing will be an encouragement for every believer.

I. **Recognizing Discouragement**
   A. Discouragement Factor Number One: Fatigue
   B. Discouragement Factor Number Two: Frustration
   C. Discouragement Factor Number Three: Failure
   D. Discouragement Factor Number Four: Fear

II. **Responding to Discouragement**
   A. Cry Out to God
   B. Continue the Work God has Given You to Do
   C. Concentrate on the Big Picture
   D. Claim the Encouragement of God's Promises
   E. Carry Somebody Else's Burden

OVERVIEW

In this lesson we encounter another of the spiritual giants whose shadow falls across the landscape of the church—the giant of discouragement. Because the Bible is filled with stories about real people facing real challenges—people like you and me—we encounter discouragement in Scripture. Thankfully, God allowed the writing down of stories that we can relate to right where we live. Stories like Nehemiah's give us hope that, while discouragement may come our way, we do not have to live with it. We can learn to overcome the giant of discouragement.

Here's the setting for what the Bible tells us of the life of Nehemiah: Seventy years before we meet him, Israel had been conquered by Babylon and taken into captivity. Then Babylon was conquered by Persia. The Persian king, Cyrus, gave the Jewish captives permission to return to their homeland and rebuild it. First to return was Zerubbabel who led a group to begin rebuilding the temple. Next came a priest by the name of Ezra and an administrator named Nehemiah.

As a priest, Ezra set about to build up the hearts of the returned captives, while Nehemiah focused on rebuilding Jerusalem's walls. By the time we get to Nehemiah, chapter four, we find Nehemiah has organized the people into efficient crews of laborers who are hard at work on the walls. They were about halfway finished rebuilding the walls when opposition to the project surfaced (Nehemiah 4:6). Two leaders in particular, Sanballat the Horonite and Tobiah the Ammonite (people who had exercised some control in the land in the Israelites' absence) rose up against Nehemiah and his project. They did everything in their power to discourage Nehemiah, to cause him to abandon his task. They didn't want the Israelites to be reestablished in the land and regain their former power and glory.

Anytime you're halfway through a project you are a prime candidate for discouragement. You're tired from what you've done and wondering if the end is actually attainable. When the people began to hear Tobiah's and Sanballat's words and warnings directed toward Nehemiah, they began to grow discouraged as well. What was Nehemiah to do? How did he defeat discouragement in his own life and keep hundreds and hundreds of his fellow Israelites from throwing up their hands in despair as well?

The lessons we will learn from the life of Nehemiah will keep us from giving in to the giant of discouragement. By the end of this lesson, you'll have learned from Nehemiah how to guard your own heart and mind. You'll have learned how to stay encouraged.

RECOGNIZING DISCOURAGEMENT

Recognizing what makes us vulnerable to discouragement is the best way to keep it at a distance.

Discouragement Factor Number One: Fatigue

In verse 10 of Nehemiah, chapter four, we learn that the "strength of the laborers [was] failing." Because we know the wall was finished in 52 days (Nehemiah 6:15), they must have been working non-stop for nearly a month when the opposition surfaced. Twenty-five or 30 days of hard work with little rest would have left the entire work force fatigued.

Someone has said that fatigue makes cowards of us all. I've seen it happen to me—perhaps you have as well. We are absolutely more vulnerable to discouragement when we are tired. I have had to acknowledge as I have gotten older that I simply can't push myself as hard as I once could. And when I try to, I quickly become unproductive. I've recognized that my basic personality type—do more, accomplish more—is probably not going to change at this point. But what I have learned to change is the way I work. When I'm working, I still work hard as we all should. But I've learned to take time to rest and recuperate. Instead of those breaks keeping me from accomplishing work, they actually enable me to do more in the long run. It's a matter of living life like a marathon instead of a sprint. As a result, I find I keep the giant of discouragement from interfering with accomplishing my goals.

Discouragement Factor Number Two: Frustration

Not only was the strength of the workers failing, but there was so much rubbish in the way from the prior wall's destruction that they could hardly work (verse 10).

You can imagine the scene—huge piles of stone blocks piled everywhere from when the Babylonians had knocked down the walls to capture the city. Sometimes laying the foundation for a project can be the most frustrating part. While it's perhaps the most important part, it's not nearly as much fun to clear the site and get ready to build as it is to see the walls rising. Moving the mountains of debris could easily have produced mountains of frustration.

There are three ways to live life: live out, wear out, or burn out. While I hope to live out, as you probably do too, some people think burning out is more spiritual. But it is not. People get burned out because they work hard without focus, purpose, or accomplishment. I know people who work incredibly hard all the time, but they never burn out because they are reaching their goals and living with a tremendous sense of accomplishment. Burning out comes from trying to accomplish something that is unattainable or at least appears that way from where you stand. Trying to build a wall on top of piles of rubble could easily lead to burnout.

Burnout could be synonymous with frustration, and frustration is an early warning sign for the onset of discouragement. It's easy for people who are tired and frustrated to conclude they are going to fail.

Discouragement Factor Number Three: Failure

Finally in verse 10 we see the potential for failure that had set in: "We are not able to build the wall." It's easy to see why they would think they might fail, being exhausted and hemmed in by rubble on every side when they were just halfway done. You can imagine the workers beginning to talk among themselves as they worked, fueling the fires of failure with their discouraging and frustrating words.

Failure itself is a giant which all of us face at some point in our lives (we will devote an entire lesson to failure in our study). We have to remember that, in a fallen world, failure is part of life. Failing is not the issue, but what we do when we fail is. How we respond to failure, as well as how we respond to exhaustion and frustration, is what makes the difference regarding discouragement.

If, when we fail, we allow the final stepping stone to discouragement—fear—to be laid, we have made a way for this giant to walk right in.

Discouragement Factor Number Four: Fear

In verses 11 and 12 those working on the walls get word of their adversaries' plans: They mean to put the Jews to death. Those who opposed the rebuilding of the walls were coming in among the Israelites and whispering in their ears, "We're going to get you."

We shouldn't be surprised at that sort of tactic resulting in fear. Relentless criticism from one's enemies can begin to take its toll over time. Occasionally I receive a critical letter from someone who has heard me speak or read something I've written. It seems that those letters always arrive at the most inopportune time. You may be struggling already and you open the mail and discover someone is out to get you (not literally, but with words). And you start believing the criticism, wondering if you ought even to continue the work you're trying to accomplish. Criticism (threats in Nehemiah's case) can lead to fear, and fear can definitely lead to discouragement.

So . . . how do we respond when we are tired, frustrated, on the verge of failure, and fearful about the future? How do we keep from getting stuck in the slough of discouragement?

RESPONDING TO DISCOURAGEMENT

Let's follow the order of events in Nehemiah, chapter four, to see how Nehemiah handled the pending possibility of serious discouragement.

Cry Out to God

The first thing he did, which is often the last thing we do, was cry out to God (verses 4, 9). How often we find ourselves saying, "We've nothing left to do but pray." Instead of ending up praying, we ought to begin by praying.

The first place to begin when discouragement sets in is prayer, to ask God to intervene in the issues at hand. Often, when I am on the verge of discouragement, I will sit down at my computer or with my journal and write out my thoughts to the Lord as a prayer. Writing out my concerns helps me identify and crystallize the issues, helps me to focus and prioritize what has become a swirl of conflicting thoughts and feelings. But in the process of writing I am also crying out to the Lord. That is always the place to begin.

Next, I turn to the Psalms of the Old Testament and encourage you to do so as well. We can think of the Psalms as the journal entries of David and the other psalmists. We get to peek into their journals and read their most intimate thoughts when they were going through times of discouragement. They become our mentors, our teachers, in learning how to cry out to God when we are discouraged.

Continue the Work God Has Given You to Do

Next, in verse six, we find that they kept working in spite of the looming opposition. It is so easy to throw in the towel when we get discouraged. We want to rid ourselves of what we think is causing the frustration and discouragement. Ironically, by giving up we separate ourselves from the one thing that can help us overcome discouragement: achieving what we set out to do. When discouraging and accusing words came against Nehemiah, he continued doing exactly what he was doing before the attacks started! He didn't let the opposition keep him from accomplishing what he set out to do.

On one occasion Nehemiah's enemies tried to entice Nehemiah to come down off the wall and meet with them in a conference. I love Nehemiah's response. He replied to his enemies that he wasn't about to leave the great work he was doing and waste time meeting with them (Nehemiah 6:3)! What was he saying? He was sending a message of commitment and determination to finish what He knew God had called him to do.

The longer I live the more I realize that when I feel least like doing something, that is the time I most need to do it. Whether it's praying, exercising, resting, reading the Bible—whatever it is, there will always be times when we won't feel encouraged about the prospects of that activity being beneficial. But it will be. And we need to do it most at the time we feel least like doing it.

Concentrate On the Big Picture

In verses 13 and 14, Nehemiah rallies the workers to continue their work in light of a bigger picture. They weren't just stacking blocks, nor were they just building a little section of a wall. Rather, they were building a huge wall that would enclose the city of Jerusalem and protect themselves and their families from those seeking to do them harm.

Sometimes, working in our little corner of the kingdom, it's easy to get discouraged. We wonder if what we're doing is making any difference or whether it's worth the trouble to continue on. Nehemiah's workers were in danger of isolation, not being able to see around the pile of rubble between them and the next group of workers further down the line. So Nehemiah positioned the workers so they could see better, could keep in touch with one another, and remain encouraged in their work. Discouragement often comes when we lose sight of the big picture. We need to stay connected to a larger community of faith so we don't lose heart.

Leith Anderson, in his book *Leadership that Works* (Bethany Publishing House, 1999) helps Christian leaders in the same way. He cites page after page of highly encouraging facts and statistics about the progress of the gospel around the world—and in America. Many people don't realize that more people attend church in America each week than attend major sporting events in a year in our country. They also don't realize that there are nearly twice as many people in their twenties in church each Sunday than in their seventies. We've been led to believe that the church isn't making an impact when it really is. It encourages us to stay focused on the big picture.

Claim the Encouragement of God's Promises

In verse 14 Nehemiah challenges the people to ". . . not be afraid of [their enemies]. Remember the Lord, great and awesome. . . ." The promises of God are the bedrock of our faith. When we are toying with discouragement and entertaining things in our mind that are not true, we need nothing more than the truth from God. And His Word is where we go to find it. Take your Bible out, plant yourself in a chair, and start reading—out loud if necessary. Sometimes I will purpose before God to keep reading His Word until He comes and speaks to my heart in a way that helps me see through my discouragement. And He always does.

The Word of God tells us not to get discouraged in the midst of the good we are doing (Galatians 6:9). Taking admonition like that to heart consistently is a powerful antidote to discouragement in life and ministry.

Carry Somebody Else's Burden

Finally, in verses 16-23 we find something very interesting taking place: people helping people. Some people were carrying, some were guarding, some were building—and all with swords strapped on. They even stayed up all night to continue the work (verses 22-23). What happens in that kind of environment? Teamwork, camaraderie, and community develop when we work together. The sharing of tasks keeps us dependent on one another. It's easier to do your part of a task than to try to do the whole thing by yourself. It's also much easier for synergy to create something "bigger than the sum of its parts" when everyone works together.

Many have been the times when I have been lifted out of discouragement by getting involved in helping someone else. When I focus on others I stop focusing on myself; and I discover in the process that others relieve their discouragement by reaching out to me. We reap what we sow (Galatians 6:7), and sowing encouragement into others' lives means we will reap it ourselves in time.

We live in potentially discouraging days. But arresting discouragement before it ever gets on the property of our heart and mind will keep it from taking over and stopping the work God is doing in and through us.

APPLICATION

1. Read 2 Corinthians 4:1-18.
   a. Humanly speaking, it would have been easy for the apostle Paul to grow discouraged in his ministry. What does he cite as being his fundamental reason for not losing heart? (verse 1)

   b. Mercy means being spared from what we deserve. Why would the receipt of mercy be a source of encouragement?

   c. What was the task Paul stayed focused on in his life? (verse 2)

   d. How did he reconcile "failures" in his preaching ministry? (verses 3-4)

   e. How did he separate himself personally from the task

   f. God had given him? (verse 5)

   g. Explain how the following phrase could be a source of encouragement for the Christian: "I obey my calling and leave the results to God."

   h. How did Paul know he was involved in something worth remaining committed to? (verse 6)

   i. How can our human tendency to grow discouraged ultimately serve to glorify God? (verse 7)

   j. Fill in the following responses Paul had to his daily experiences: (verses 8-9)

      (1) Hard pressed but not . . .

      (2) Perplexed but not . . .

(3) Persecuted but not . . .

(4) Struck down but not . . .

k. Why did Paul never lose heart (grow discouraged) in ministry? (verse 16-17)

l. What did he stay focused on? (verse 18)

2. Read 2 Corinthians 5:1-10.
   a. How did Paul express the reality of living life in a fallen world? (verses 1-4)

   b. How did faith play a role in Paul avoiding discouragement? (verse 7)

   c. How would discouragement have affected his life goal? (verse 9)

   d. What future event constantly served as a reminder to Paul of his responsibility to stay encouraged and pursuing the call of God on his life? (verse 10)

3. How is it possible to get discouraged even when we are doing good?

   a. What admonition does Paul give to those who are at work doing good things? (Galatians 6:9; II Thessalonians 3:13)

   b. What good work do you consistently in which you find yourself tempted to discouragement?

   c. List the reasons why you are tempted to grow discouraged in the midst of that good work and the truth from God's Word that can keep you encouraged:

   Temptation   Truth

d. What is the ultimate reason for continuing to sow seeds of encouragement into your life as well as into the lives of others? (Galatians 6:7)

DID YOU KNOW?

To encourage means to impart courage, as in a blood transfusion. When you encourage someone you give them a transfusion of courage. But what does it mean to encourage oneself? In that case, think of the actions of a farmer who burns his field in order to remove the stubble and encourage new growth. Or the gardener who prunes a plant to encourage the multiplication of fruit. Sometimes self-encouragement means being ruthless with the fears, failures, frustration, and fatigue which can discourage us. We may have to give ourselves a transfusion of courage by cleansing ourselves of whatever is standing in the way of encouragement. If no one comes along to encourage you, encourage yourself. That's what David did—"Why are you cast down, O my soul? . . . Hope in God . . . ." (Psalm 42:11).

FACING THE GIANT OF LONELINESS

Selected Scriptures

In this lesson we confront the reality of loneliness and learn how to avoid its negative effects.

OUTLINE

The poet has said, "No man is an island," yet we often feel as though we are. Life has a way of setting us aside or separating us from others at times. Our challenge is to learn to take the steps back to connectedness, steps that keep us from being lonely for any length of time.

I. **The Experience of Loneliness**
   A. The Lonely Single
   B. The Lonely Spouse
   C. The Lonely Survivor
   D. The Lonely Senior Citizen
   E. The Lonely Sufferer
   F. The Lonely Servant of God

II. **The Examples of Loneliness in the Bible**
   A. David the King
   B. Jeremiah the Prophet
   C. Paul the Apostle

III. **The Escape from Loneliness**
   A. Acknowledge the Reality of Your Loneliness
   B. Accept God's Provision for Your Loneliness
   C. Allow God's Word to Fill Your Heart and Mind
   D. Activate Your Network of Christian Friends

OVERVIEW

In his book *Six Hours One Friday* (Multnomah Press, 1989), author Max Lucado writes about taking a walk through an old cemetery in his hometown. Many of the graves were of people who lived and died in the 19th century. Many of the names belonged to children, bearing witness to the difficulties of life on the Texas prairie.

One grave he came across struck him sharply. It had no dates of birth or death, just the name of a woman and her two husbands. The epitaph on the grave read simply,

> Sleeps but rests not.
> Loved but was loved not.
> Tried to please, but pleased not.
> Died as she lived—alone.

What a sad testimony, to have lived and died alone. We tend to think life among the pioneers and settlers might have been more lonely than our lives. No telephones or dependable mail system, no neighbors close by to keep company with. But the truth is just the opposite. Loneliness has reached epidemic proportions in our modern world. Even though we have a half-dozen ways to communicate with the outside world at our fingertips, people today are lonelier than they have ever been in history.

Because loneliness creates a feeling of emptiness on the inside, people try to compensate for that feeling by filling themselves with food, drugs, alcohol, material things, sex, work, or other peoples' lives. Loneliness is not removed by substitutes for true relationships in life—the most foundational being our relationship with God. Everyone experiences loneliness at different times in life, and it is not always a bad or dangerous experience. There is something to be said for learning to be alone with ourselves and God. But loneliness over the long term can have negative effects physically as well as spiritually.

In this lesson we'll talk about the experience of loneliness in life, we'll study some characters in Scripture who experienced loneliness, and we'll learn how to escape the negative effects of loneliness.

THE EXPERIENCE OF LONELINESS

Different stages of our lives result in different kinds of loneliness. As you read through this lesson you'll no doubt identify with one or more of these significant times of loneliness.

The Lonely Single

The extended community in which I reside, San Diego, California, has one of the largest single populations in the United States. Whether it's for the beautiful weather, the California lifestyle, the many entrepreneurial ventures, or the military bases, young single adults flock to San Diego. I know from my own relationships with single Christians that going home to an empty house or apartment night after night can be a lonely lifestyle. And this is true not only in my community, but everywhere. The burgeoning singles bar and club scene in America is just one indication of how desperate many single people are to conquer loneliness by meeting someone—anyone—to talk to. Being a Christian helps—a single believer in Christ has spiritual resources to draw on in times of loneliness. But human beings were not created by God to spend their life alone (Genesis 2:18). And by that I don't mean marriage exclusively—but in the presence of other people.

The Lonely Spouse

It is an amazement to me that the institution God created to provide the greatest sense of intimacy often becomes a place of great loneliness. I remember speaking somewhere on this topic and receiving a letter in the mail the next week from a woman who had heard my message. She wrote, "Today you really struck a spot that is sensitive in my heart. I try not to dwell on it—the loneliness in marriage, but the truth is I am lonely. My husband and I are both Christians. We live relatively well. We are educated, and my husband is a good man. He works hard and is a good provider. He isn't abusive, and he is a fairly good father. But my emotional needs are very rarely met because he works all the time. It's the case of two people living parallel lives but never really meeting at all. He has heard and read a little about how a husband can create a good relationship with his wife, but it must all pass over him without making an impression. . . . I try not to think about it. But the hurt is deep. I am a very lonely person."

It is sad that the very relationship God ordained to combat loneliness has become for many the most lonely place on earth.

The Lonely Survivor

Then there are the lonely survivors, the spouses who live on after a loved one has died. Lonely survivors experience a kind of pain which, I am told, is so intense that there is nothing in life to which it can be compared. Not having gone through that loss personally I can only imagine what it must be like. While the death of a spouse is heart-rending, at least it comes with a sense of closure. Divorce is another kind of loneliness producer that is perhaps even worse, for there is no finality. It is an open wound that rarely heals completely. Not only is there physical and emotional loneliness to contend with but a sense of rejection as well.

The Lonely Senior Citizen

The number of senior citizens in our country is growing at a faster rate than at any time in history. The sense of loneliness that sets in with seniors is significant. Often they have lost a spouse, their children have moved away, and they struggle to find a place to fit in where they can feel significant. The position of authority, influence, and respect they occupied in their vocational years is no longer theirs, and so their loneliness is one of significance as much as personal contact. For today's seniors, the sense of loneliness that comes from a loss of significance is often the most acute kind of loneliness there is. Searching for, and finding, a purpose in the twilight years of life is a great challenge.

The Lonely Sufferer

There is the lonely sufferer who experiences the pain he cannot describe to anyone else. Sometimes that loneliness is in a busy place like a hospital. One man wrote to me from his hospital bed: "It is when the lights go out and the room is suddenly plunged into darkness that the awful awareness comes. The traffic of the hospital goes on like an uncontrolled fever outside my door. But inside, the room is so still. Loneliness can be compounded by suffering. Many suffer physically or emotionally in ways that cannot be described or be cured instantly. The loneliness Job felt was not just because he had lost his family but because he was suffering physically in the midst of his loss.

The Lonely Servant of God

What can I say about the person who leaves his familiar culture and goes to the mission field, leaving behind everything and everyone that kept him from being lonely? He goes into a brand new culture where everything is different—food, language, customs—and he doesn't know anyone on a personal level. It takes far more time to establish new relationships because of the cultural barriers which must be overcome. We get letters from missionaries in which you can read tales of loneliness written between the lines. They are not complaining—but you can tell they are paying a price for their service to God on a foreign mission field.

Leadership can be a lonely place. Moses said, "I cannot carry all these people by myself; the burden is too heavy for me" (Numbers 11:14). Anyone who has ever been in a position of leadership knows that it can be lonely "at the top." When a leader moves out ahead of those he is leading, he is turning his back on those who follow. You can be the leader of a large church or a large ministry organization and still experience loneliness. It comes with the territory.

We can find great heroes of the faith in Scripture who experienced loneliness in their lives. It is not a sin to be lonely, for great men and women of God have battled loneliness. We can develop a sinful response to loneliness, but it is not a sin to experience those feelings from time to time. Seeing that others have been lonely can make us know that we are not alone in our feelings.

THE EXAMPLES OF LONELINESS IN THE BIBLE

David the King

David wrote on one occasion, "For my days are consumed like smoke, And my bones are burned like a hearth. . . . I am like a pelican of the wilderness; I am like an owl of the desert. I lie awake,

And am like a sparrow alone on the housetop" (Psalm 102:3, 6-7). You can almost feel the edge of David's pain as he describes his feelings. David was hounded all over the Judean wilderness by King Saul, a fugitive for much of his pre-royal life. When I read about David's loneliness, it comforts and instructs me to know that he survived and trusted God in the midst of it.

Jeremiah the Prophet

The story of Jeremiah the prophet is one of the most agonizing stories you will ever read. Jeremiah was also the author of the book of Lamentations, a collection of funeral dirges expressing the anguish of his heart as he watched the city of Jerusalem go down in ruin before his very eyes. Jeremiah is known as the weeping prophet because of the tears he shed over the destruction of God's city. No one would listen to his calls for repentance whereby the city might be saved. He was a lonely voice crying out in a spiritual wilderness. He finally confessed that he would be better off leaving and going out into the dessert than to remain among those who cared so little for God (Jeremiah 9:2). For him, the loneliness of the wilderness would have been better than the loneliness he felt among his own people.

Paul the Apostle

Paul wrote most of the New Testament, founded missionary churches all over the Mediterranean world, and penned the greatest theological treatise of all time in the letter to the Romans. Would someone like Paul suffer from loneliness? On occasion he did.

At the end of the last letter he wrote before he died, addressed to his protégé Timothy, he found himself in a Roman prison. This was not the setting of his first arrest in Rome which was more like a house-arrest (Acts 28:30). This time, he was imprisoned in a Roman dungeon where his friends even had a hard time locating him (2 Timothy 1:6, 17; 2:9; 4:13). Listen to the words he wrote to Timothy which give evidence of his loneliness: "Be diligent to come to me quickly; for Demas has forsaken me, having loved this present world, and has departed for Thessalonica—Crescens for Galatia, Titus for Dalmatia. Only Luke is with me . . . . And Tychicus I have sent to Ephesus . . . . Alexander the coppersmith did me much harm . . . . At my first defense no one stood with me, but all forsook me. May it not be charged against them" (2 Timothy 4:9-16).

Do you feel that? Here is the great apostle, standing alone at the end of his life. No one is with him. You would think that could not happen after all he had done for the church, but it did. We sense no resentment in Paul's words, only the fact of his aloneness.

When loneliness sweeps over you like a wave, remember you are not the first person to have been lonely, and not the first Christian. As I have said, it is no sin to be lonely. But it can become a sin if we indulge it and allow it to turn to self-pity. God has given us ways to escape from loneliness before it becomes a downward spiral that pulls us down with it.

THE ESCAPE FROM LONELINESS

Here are four ways to defend yourself from the power of loneliness:

Acknowledge the Reality of Your Loneliness

Christians have made an art of denying the reality of some parts of life. Because it seems unspiritual to confess to being lonely, many Christians will quote Hebrews 13:5, where Christ said, "I will never leave you nor forsake you," and profess they are never lonely because He is always with them. Theologically it is true that Christ is always with the believer, but our practice doesn't always match our position. It is more honest, transparent, and real to simply say, "Yes, I am lonely at this time of my life," than to deny the reality of our situation. Human beings experience loneliness at times, and there is no shame in a Christian admitting that fact.

Accept God's Provision for Your Loneliness

Ultimately, God's provision for loneliness is the only suitable solution. There is a fundamental emptiness in every human being which can only be filled by the presence of God Himself. It is interesting to note that the only time Jesus Christ cried out in loneliness was from the cross when the Father forsook Him and allowed Him to die as a sacrifice for the world. Without the presence of God, the most agonizing loneliness will afflict even the strongest person. No person should search for a solution for his loneliness without solving the basic issue of separation from God. Accepting Jesus Christ, and being filled by His Spirit, is the first step toward overcoming the negative dimensions of loneliness.

Allow God's Word to Fill Your Heart and Mind

I say this so frequently that it can be misinterpreted as a Christian platitude. But it is not. I say it often because it is the absolute truth! Second only to the presence of God's Spirit in one's life is the presence of God's Word as an antidote to loneliness. God has spoken clearly, and if you read His Word you will hear His voice.

Activate Your Network of Christian Friends

Let me close with a strong word, strong because it is true: Living in the house of loneliness is a choice. You may not have become lonely by choice, but remaining lonely is something you don't have to do. The body of Christ exists to encourage and strengthen Christians, but if we refuse to get involved it is difficult for that to happen. Each believer must assume the responsibility for his own emotional and spiritual health, including not lingering in loneliness. In the average church there are numerous "doors" through which one can enter into relationships of service and friendship. But you must walk through the door.

It is no sin to be lonely. But if you are, move purposefully toward overcoming the negative effects of loneliness. No one else can do as much for you as you can do for yourself by taking that step.

APPLICATION

1. Read Hebrews 13:56.
   a. What does Hebrews 13:5b contribute to your understanding of avoiding long-term loneliness?

   b. What about Matthew 28:20b?

   c. Why do we still feel lonely at times even though Christ has promised to always be with us?

   d. What is the root of loneliness for the Christian? Is it the absence of divine fellowship or human fellowship?

   e. What is the root of loneliness for the non-Christian?

   f. If loneliness as we usually describe it is predominantly in the human dimension, what impact does the presence of God have? That is, does God impact our loneliness at all?

2. In what way(s) have you experienced loneliness in your life?

   a. How did you respond to the situation? Did you take steps to counteract the effects of your loneliness?

   b. What difference did being a Christian make? What impact did the presence of God have on your feelings of loneliness?

   c. Have you discovered ongoing, predictable situations in which you are vulnerable to loneliness?

   d. What measures do you take ahead of time to guard against the negative effects of being alone?

3. Read Ecclesiastes 4:9-12.
   a. What is the central message of this passage?

   b. What is the "good reward for their labor"? (verse 9b)

   c. What are the three examples of ways people in Biblical cultures helped each other? (verses 10-12)

   d. In terms of loneliness, what are the ways two are better than one?

e. How many people do you know whom you could count on as described in these verses?

f. When is the last time you called on another person for help or companionship in order to combat feelings of loneliness?

g. What kind of loneliness were you feeling?

h. Is your relationship with this friend such that you can share your feelings of loneliness?

i. How were they able to help?

j. When is the last time you reached out to a person whom you feared was being overtaken by feelings of loneliness? How were you able to help?

k. Given the number of "one another" passages in the New Testament, should anyone in the body of Christ ever be lonely for a significant length of time? (e.g., Romans 12:5; 13:8; 15:5, 14; 1 Corinthians 12:25; Galatians 5:13; Ephesians 4:25)

4. Read Ephesians 4:15-16.
   a. What does verse 16 have to say about loneliness in the body of Christ?

   b. How does not getting involved in the body of Christ impact the individual?

   c. How does it impact the rest of the body of Christ?

DID YOU KNOW?

It's wise to prepare to be lonely. If you know there are certain times of the week or year that you tend to experience loneliness, prepare for those times in advance. If you do, you'll be following a good example—that of Jesus Christ Himself. Approaching the most difficult night of His life, when He would be apprehended by Roman soldiers, Jesus took His three closest friends with Him to the Garden of Gethsemane. He asked them just to be with Him while He went to pray. Unfortunately, their example was lacking as they fell asleep! But Jesus' example is one worth following: prepare for those times when you may experience waves of loneliness by planning on being involved with friends or extended family. Conquer loneliness before it has a chance to conquer you.

FACING THE GIANT OF WORRY

Matthew 6:25-34

In this lesson we are introduced to the folly of worry and how to avoid it.

OUTLINE

Worry is concern over the future. But, the future is not here. Only God sees the shape of it. And according to the Bible, worry is concern over the unknown—the uncontrollable future. Prepare to face the giant of worry by finding out what Jesus us talking about, and what He is not talking about, when He says in the Sermon on the Mount, "Don't Worry."

I.   **Facing the Giant of Worry**
   A. Worry is Inconsistent
   B. Worry is Irrational
   C. Worry is Ineffective
   D. Worry is Illogical
   E. Worry is Irreligious

II. **Fighting the Giant of Worry**
   A. To Win Over Worry We Need a System of Priorities
   B. To Win Over Worry We Need a Strategic Program

OVERVIEW

A t the very moment you are reading the words on this page, you are probably (if you're like most people) worried about something! You might disagree, saying you are "concerned." But that's another of the code words we Christians use when we don't want to admit that we're doing what we shouldn't. Let's face it—everyone finds themselves facing the huge giant of worry at times. And that's where we've arrived in our study of the giants we face in our spiritual experience.

Corrie Ten Boom used to say, "Worry is an old man with bended head, carrying a load of feathers which he thinks are lead." That's a beautiful, non-technical definition of worry—being anxious about something that doesn't exist in fact but that we believe does or might exist. The New Testament word for worry is translated by the phrase "to take thought" or "to be careful." It comes from a Greek word which means to have a divided mind. So to be a worrier is to have your mind divided between legitimate thoughts and thoughts that are not legitimate, thoughts which you shouldn't be thinking.

Worry is future-focused. The person who worries has two problems: The future is not here and the future is not his. Worrying cannot change the future nor can it control the future. Jesus said it was wrong to worry. In His words in Matthew 6:25-34 (our text for this lesson), three times He said, "Don't worry." Those words give us our marching orders for defeating the giant of worry.

Before we study Jesus' words, let me tell you what "Don't worry" doesn't mean. First, it doesn't mean, "Don't plan." The King James Version of Matthew 6:34 says, "Take therefore no thought for the morrow." That almost sounds like, "Don't think about tomorrow," which is not what it means. Jesus, Himself certainly planned, and the Scriptures support the idea of being responsible in our approach to the future. Not worrying is not the same as not planning.

Second, Jesus is not saying, "Don't ever be concerned." We are not to float through life on a breeze of indifference, ignoring the realities around us. There are plenty of things in life to be morally, spiritually, and practically concerned about as a Christian. But not worrying is not the same thing as not being concerned.

So, when Jesus says, "Don't worry," He doesn't mean "Don't plan" and He doesn't mean "Don't be concerned." He means don't get so exercised about that over which you have no control that you paralyze yourself and those who depend on you. Worry and anxiety change nothing except the worrier—and it's always in negative ways.

FACING THE GIANT OF WORRY (6:25-32)

We will divide Jesus' words about worry into two sections. In verses 25-32 we will discover why worry is a fruitless endeavor.

Worry Is Inconsistent (6:25)

It doesn't make sense to conclude that God has already done the biggest job (creating our body, our life) but then would fail to do the smaller job (providing what we need to live the life He has given us). It is an argument from the greater to the lesser. God obviously knew what it would take for bodies like ours to exist—food, clothing, and shelter. It is completely inconsistent with the wise and loving character of God to think that He did the one thing without also doing the other. When we worry about our future provision of food, clothing, and shelter, we actually malign the character of our God. Our bodies, our very lives, are clear evidence that God is a creator and provider. For Him not to feed, clothe, and shelter that which He has created doesn't make sense.

Worry Is Irrational (6:26)

Verse 26 shows how irrational worry is. Verse 25 dealt with the question of whether God is able to provide. The answer is "Yes" since He has already done the harder job of creating life. Now Jesus takes up the question: "Will He provide?" Whereas He argued from the greater to the lesser in verse 25, here He speaks from the lesser to the greater: "If God provides for something as simple as the birds of the air, won't He also provide for you?" It's irrational to think that He wouldn't.

In Matthew 10:29-31 Jesus says that two sparrows can be bought for a copper coin, and Luke 12:6 says that five sparrows can be bought for two coins. So it appears that the market for sparrows was like this: Buy two for a penny, but if you buy four they throw in a fifth sparrow for free. Jesus is saying that not even the most inexpensive and smallest parts of God's creation change their status without it being part of His will (not even the hairs on our head! Matthew 10:30). Therefore, if tiny things like sparrows and hair are under His watchful eye and concern, how much more are we who are the pinnacle of His creation. Will He care for us? The answer is: "Of course He will!"

Worry Is Ineffective (6:27)

Not only is worry inconsistent and irrational, it is also ineffective. Verse 27 asks, "How can worrying add anything to your life? Answer: It can't. Worry is totally ineffective when it comes to improving or changing your prospects for the future.

Jesus uses the cubit as an illustration to make His point. A cubit was the standard unit of measure in Biblical days, equal to about 18 inches in length. Jesus asks, in essence, "How many of you can sit there in a chair and worry all day about your height and add 18 inches to it?" The answer is, again, no one. You could worry all day and not change one thing about yourself—except make your hair a bit more gray!

It's likely that Jesus meant something deeper than just the issue of height. It's possible that He was referring to the length of one's life: Who, by worrying, can add any length to his life? And, of course, the answer is no one. In fact, the opposite is probably true. Cemeteries are no doubt filled with people whose lives were shortened by worry. Doctors are discovering more and more negative effects of worry, stress, anger, and anxiety on the human body. Instead of lengthening your life, worry might shorten it. Worry doesn't change tomorrow, but it sure changes today. Worry robs you of the strength and ability to enjoy the gift of life today that God wants you to enjoy.

Worry Is Illogical (6:28-30)

The fourth fallacy of worry is that it is illogical. Jesus next turns to nature, the beautiful lilies of the field which God has clothed in glorious splendor—and does so year after year. We know far more about the beauty of nature today than was apparent in Biblical days. We have discovered unbelievable beauty in the flora and fauna of this earth which are even more astounding than lilies. Therefore, the point Jesus makes here should be even more obvious to us today than it was to His disciples.

Solomon was the richest, and therefore the most beautifully dressed sovereign in the world. Yet even Solomon's golden glory could not compare with the delicate beauty of the flowers of the field who are clothed effortlessly by God every spring. Is it logical to think that God, who clothes the flowers in splendor, will not also clothe those whom He has created? No, it is completely illogical.

Jesus' argument is based on nature, that which God Himself took the initiative to create and "clothe." If mankind is the pinnacle of creation (Psalm 8), we should expect that God would assume the responsibility for providing for our clothing as well.

Worry Is Irreligious (6:31-32)

The final fault to be found with worry is that it betrays our spiritual heritage. In verses 31 and 32, Jesus compares those within Israel who worry about the future to the Gentiles. This is not to be a put down of non-Jewish people. Rather it is a statement about religious heritage. Gentiles were the pagans or heathens of the world who were either idolaters or atheists. They either worshipped wood and stone idols or no god at all. In that case, they had every right to be worried about the future.

But for those who claim to have a personal relationship with the Creator God of heaven and earth, worrying is a complete contradiction of what we say we believe. To worry is to act like there is no God who has promised to take care of us. That doesn't mean that Christians don't have momentary worries. Ask any parent who has raised teenagers, and you'll discover that worries are a consistent part of life. But the key is to take a momentary worry and use it as a springboard to a mature, spiritual response. Meeting worry is okay; moving in with worry is not. When we make worry our constant companion we betray our spiritual heritage.

But Jesus doesn't rebuke us. Notice how tenderly He concludes this section: "Your heavenly Father knows that you need all these things." Jesus knows that worry is a liability of living in this fallen world. But He wants us to learn that worry is a leaky boat, incapable of transporting us safely to the shore of the future. There is a safer way to get there—defeat the giant of worry by seeking God's kingdom and righteousness above all.

FIGHTING THE GIANT OF WORRY (6:33-34)

To defeat the giant of worry, two things are needed: priorities for today and a plan for yesterday and tomorrow.

To Win Over Worry We Need a System of Priorities (6:33)

Much of the worry that destroys people is the worry of a divided heart. A divided heart cannot decide what it believes and therefore how it is going to live. It gets caught up in every wind of change that blows through society. A person without priorities will constantly find his heart captured by (and worrying about) everything that "might" be.

Jesus said to focus in on only one thing in life: the kingdom of God and the values which it stands for. When we do that, everything else in life will fall into place according to the will of God and according to His provision. The King takes care of those who dwell in His kingdom.

Many Christians who worry do so because they know they have violated the priority of seeking God first. Not only do they worry about the future, they worry about worrying about the future! Worry becomes a cycle they cannot break. The only way to stop it is to jump off the merry-go-round of worry and ask, "What is the most important, thing to me?" If you conclude that God is most important you are ready to make a clean break with worry. Making God your priority will prepare you for developing a strategy for dealing with the yesterdays and tomorrows you used to worry about.

To Win Over Worry We Need a Strategic Program (6:34)

The final verse in this section holds what may be the key truth in understanding how to defeat the giant of worry: focus on today. No one ever sank under the burdens of today; but add yesterday and tomorrow to today, and it can capsize your life. Jesus said, "Sufficient for the day is its own trouble."

Dr. Osler, a famous physician of years past, made a helpful observation. He noted how ocean going vessels were able to seal off various sections of the boat so that a leak could be contained in only one part of the ship. Though damaged, a ship could still make it to safety. Just so, he suggested, we need to develop the capacity for sealing off the yesterdays and tomorrows that fuel the fires of worry. We need to learn to live in the compartment of today alone.

1. Do Not Dwell on Your Tomorrows

What Jesus teaches in verse 34 probably has its roots in Deuteronomy 33:25b: "As your days, so shall your strength be." That is, you will have strength from God as the events of your days require. As a pastor, I have counseled with many families through the years who have gone through devastating financial losses. When they express concerns about their future, I can only remind them of these truths. God promises to take care of today, and we are to trust Him for that.

We need to seal off the door that keeps us from worrying about tomorrow so that tomorrow doesn't sap today of its strength and vitality. But we also need to seal off our yesterdays—those days which are already in the history books and cannot be changed.

2. Do Not Dwell on Your Yesterdays

There are three things I have discovered people worrying about when it comes to yesterday: sins, successes, and sorrows—all unchangeable.

(a) We worry about yesterday's sins

People who come to Christ out of a background stained by sin and wantonness often have a difficult time putting the memories of those things out of their minds. It is my privilege to remind such people, and all who have sinned, that God has put our sins as far from us as the east is from the west (Psalm

103:12). Or, if people agree that God has forgiven them, they say they cannot forgive themselves. In both cases, we need to allow God to seal us off from the sins of our past. The guilt and shame of them cannot leak into the compartment of today.

(b) We worry about yesterday's successes

Sometimes those who have no problem sealing off their sin don't do as well sealing off their successes. Many who come into the Christian life having reached the pinnacle of success in their vocational career have a hard time switching priorities and focus. The apostle Paul was a young Jewish scholar on the fast track to success in Pharisaism when he met Christ. He closed the door on his past successes—"forgetting those things which are behind" (Philippians 3:13)—in order to focus on Christ and His kingdom. We must learn to do the same.

(c) We worry about yesterday's sorrows

This may be the hardest. We put aside sin and success, but the sorrow that lingers after life's tragedies and heartaches is often difficult to seal off. It's like sealing off a part of our own heart and soul, the place where sorrow lives. We must learn to live in the presence of Almighty God who knew a greater sorrow than any we have ever felt. He who lost His only Son as a sacrifice to undeserved sin knows your every pain and longing. Don't deny your sorrow, but don't let it control today.

God is the great "I AM" (Exodus 3:14), not "I WAS" or "I WILL BE." The Christian who lives with Him today, in the present tense, is the one who will be free from worries about yesterday, today, or tomorrow.

APPLICATION

1. Read Romans 8:32, 38-39.
   a. In verse 32, is Paul arguing from the greater to the lesser or the lesser to the greater? Explain your answer:

   b. The greater thing God has done:

   c. The lesser things God has promised to do:

   d. How does Paul's reasoning here concerning the gift of Jesus Christ compare to Jesus' words in Matthew 6:25-34?

   e. Have you received God's gift of forgiveness of sin?

   f. What else can you expect God to faithfully provide for you?

   g. What does Paul mention in verse 38 that ties in with not worrying about past or future things?

   h. What can anything in your past, present, or future NOT do? (verse 39)

   i. How confident would you be (free from worry) if you were walking through life with Jesus Christ as the early disciples did?

   j. If you cannot be separated from Him (verse 39) what should that do for your ability to live free from worry?

2. List everything in your life that you worry continually about:

a. How would your life be different if you had no worries? (Not if you had no problems, but if you had no worries about the problems?)

b. How does God respond to your worries? (How does a parent feel if a child doesn't believe or trust him or her?)

c. What could you do today to seal off the past and the future and live with "strength for today?"

3. Read Psalm 8:3-9.
   a. Where does man rank in the order of creation?

   b. With what has God crowned man? (verse 5)

   c. What other examples of nature are mentioned that God actively provides for? (verses 7-8)

   d. How would you expect God to care for the very highest part of His creation?

4. From the following verses, describe everything God has done with your past sins:

   a. Psalm 103:12

   b. Isaiah 1:18; 38:17

   c. Jeremiah 31:34; 50:20

   d. Micah 7:18-19

   e. In light of these verses, what should you do when you recall a past sin instead of worrying about it?

5. Read 1 Peter 5:6-7.
   a. Who is in charge of all time? (verse 6)

   b. While you wait to see how God reveals His will over time, what should you do? (verse 7)

DID YOU KNOW?

E veryone thinks about the future—such as what you'll do when you finish reading this lesson. The issue is not the future; it's how we approach the future. There are only two ways: with faith or with fear. If we approach the future with faith, we walk under God's umbrella, under the protection of His provision and plan. If we approach the future with fear, we step out from under that umbrella. We invite the enemy to begin taunting and tempting us, warning us about the disasters just around the bend. The only way to avoid future shock in life is to walk by faith. The difference between worrying in fear and walking by faith is the difference between living and just being alive.

FACING THE GIANT OF GUILT

Psalms 32 and 51

In this lesson we will learn how to remove the guilt of sin.

OUTLINE

We would rather call sin anything except sin. But if we fail to call sin what God calls it—if we rationalize it or excuse it—we will lose the joy of our salvation. Confession, cleansing, and restoration is the only way to remove the guilt and shame of sin.

I. **The Agony of Guilt**
   A. Silence
   B. Sorrow
   C. Secrecy

II. **The Accusation of Guilt**

III. **The Admission of Guilt**
   A. He Accepts Full Responsibility for His Sin
   B. He Acknowledges the Sinfulness of Sin
   C. He Addresses His Confession to God

IV. **The Answer to Guilt**
   A. Removing the Sin
   B. Restoring the Joy
   C. Renewing the Fellowship

M any people don't know that King David of Israel battled two giants in his lifetime. Goliath is the well-known giant he defeated in a matter of minutes, but Guilt is the lesser-known giant it took him many months to defeat.

David met the giant named Guilt when he saw a beautiful woman from the roof of his palace and had her brought to him. He committed adultery with her and then sent her home. What he thought was going to be a simple and brief encounter became complicated when the woman, Bathsheba, sent him word that she was pregnant by him.

David knew he had to cover his sin or risk losing his reputation as a godly king. He sent for Bathsheba's husband, Uriah, who was away fighting in David's army. He figured Uriah would come home and have relations with Bathsheba, and it would then appear her pregnancy was caused by her husband, not David. But David did not plan on Uriah's loyalty and honor. Uriah refused to enjoy the comfort of his wife when his fellow soldiers were still in battle, so he spent the night outside David's palace.

When David realized his plan hadn't worked, he implemented a second plan—to have his army commander send Uriah into the heat of battle so he would be killed. And that is exactly what happened. David was then guilty of murder as well as adultery. Nine months later a child was born to Bathsheba. Through his own writings, we are introduced to David's state of mind and his actions following the birth of his child.

Two psalms—Psalms 32 and 51—give us insight into what it was like for David to live with the guilt of his sin (Psalm 32) and the confession of his sin to God (Psalm 51). Defeating Guilt, the giant of his philandering, became a far greater challenge than defeating Goliath, the giant of the Philistines.

THE AGONY OF GUILT (PSALM 32)

Psalm 32 describes in part the anguish of body and soul that David went through while concealing his sin.

Silence (32:3)

David couldn't talk to the Lord about his sin, and therefore he couldn't talk to the Lord about anything. The Bible says, "If I regard iniquity in my heart, the Lord will not hear" (Psalm 66:18). So David no longer had fellowship with God. His heart became silent. His communication with God was cut off. His guilt began to take on physiological dimensions. He said that his bones grew old through his groaning all the day long. He apparently became physically incapacitated from carrying the guilt of what he had done.

Sorrow (32:4)

He said, "For day and night Your hand was heavy upon me; My vitality was turned into the drought of summer." King David was still commanding all of his subjects as the king, but he could not command his own conscience. He was filled with agony. His freshness of life was gone, replaced with bitterness and anguish. His conscience was filled with disgust, breaking his communion with God. His life was a mess.

Secrecy

One reason he suffered so much was there was no one to whom he could convey his pain. Nobody knew what David had done except Bathsheba and Joab—and each of them only knew the half of it. His sin with Bathsheba may not have been planned, but his sin against Uriah was planned and premeditated. For over a year David tried to live with his secret guilt. He couldn't talk to God. He couldn't talk to his friends. He could only talk to himself, but he kept getting only condemnation from his own conscience. Guilt was wearing him away.

Then the Lord sent someone to help David with his problem—which brings us to the accusation of guilt.

THE ACCUSATION OF GUILT
(2 SAMUEL 12:1-7)

God sent a prophet named Nathan to confront David about his sin. The Lord apparently revealed to Nathan what he needed to know about David's sin, and Nathan decided to use a story to call David to account. It was a story of two men, one rich and one poor. When a traveler came by and needed some food, the rich man, instead of taking food from his own flocks, took the poor man's sole lamb and gave it to the traveler.

In this story, David is obviously the rich man, Uriah the poor man, and Bathsheba the lamb taken by the rich man. David has no idea Nathan is telling a story about him. He thinks this is something that actually happened in his kingdom, and he exclaimed ". . . the man who has done this shall surely die . . . because he had no pity!" (2 Samuel 12:5). Nathan then lowered the boom on David: "You are the man!"

It's hard to imagine a moment filled with more anguish and relief at the same time. While David was humiliated and ashamed, finally the secret sins he had carried for so many months were out in the open. It was now time for him to admit his guilt and move toward cleansing.

THE ADMISSION OF GUILT (PSALM 51)

We now move to Psalm 51, which says in its superscription (at the beginning of the psalm), "A Psalm of David when Nathan the prophet went to him, after he had gone in to Bathsheba." What we have in Psalm 51 is David's response to his confrontation with Nathan the prophet. In this psalm we discover the pattern for defeating the giant of guilt in our own lives.

He Accepts Full Responsibility for His Sin

Step one in defeating guilt is accepting full responsibility for sin. You might take a colored highlighter pen and go down through Psalm 51 and highlight each first person singular pronoun: I, me, my, mine. You'll get a good indication of exactly how precise David was being in his confession. He was not avoiding the fact that he was the one who had sinned and was guilty before God.

Taking responsibility for sin is almost a lost art in our day and time. We have learned to excuse and rationalize almost every conceivable act. But guilt is only removed when it is acknowledged and confessed. Sin is like a stain on a table top. You may hide it by putting a plate over it, but the stain is still there. It only comes off by removing what's hiding it and dealing with the stain itself. That's what David did.

He Acknowledges the Sinfulness of Sin (51:1-2, 4)

In three verses David uses four different words to describe what he has done: transgression, iniquity, sin, and evil. Each of these words expresses a different aspect of his breaking of God's law. When we confess our sin we are saying the same thing about it that God says about it. If we don't say the same thing God says, we haven't confessed. In Psalm 32:5 David said, "I acknowledged my sin to You, And my iniquity I have not hidden. I said, 'I will confess my transgressions to the LORD.'" That's saying it like it is.

Even in America, there was a day when people were scared of sin. They fled from it and hated it and feared that concealing it might threaten their very salvation. But today we find people using every word except "sin" to describe behavior that is offensive to God. When it comes to our sin we mumble instead of confess. We find teachers asking rebellious children how it made them feel when they stole another child's lunch money. We find the word "sin" appearing on desert menus, describing the decadence of chocolate fudge. We have so insulated ourselves against the concept of sin that our modern generation thinks nothing of living with all kinds of sins unconfessed in their lives. And the church is in danger of adopting that mentality as well. We don't need to model David's sin, but we do need to model his confession.

He Addresses His Confession to God (51:4)

Notice that he says it is ultimately against God that he has sinned. It's not that David was insensitive to the reality of the damage he had brought to other peoples' lives. He is saying that he realizes sin is first and foremost a violation of God's holy standards and that God is the one, before whom confession and repentance is due. If we go and ask another person to forgive us before we have confessed our sin to God, then we have misunderstood the priorities of confession. Of course we should ask forgiveness of the people our sin has hurt. But above all, a holy God is most offended by our sin and to Him our confession should first go.

THE ANSWER TO GUILT (PSALM 51:7-12)

There are three steps to the complete removal of sin in the sight of God and man: Remove the sin, restore the joy, and renew the fellowship.

Removing the Sin (51:2, 7, 9)

If the confession of sin is the bad news then the removal of it is the good news. And David addresses sin's removal with a variety of language equal to that which he used to describe his sin: "Wash me thoroughly . . . cleanse me . . . purge me . . . wash me . . . blot out . . ." As mentioned before, sin is like a stain. The word "cleanse" was also used to refer to the cleansing of a leper in the Old Testament. It is as if David is saying, "Cleanse the leprosy-like sin which has afflicted my soul."

When a person in Old Testament Israel came into contact with a dead body, he had to be ceremonially cleansed with hyssop. Here David says, "Purge me with hyssop . . . ," probably a reference to the death of Uriah which he caused. "Blot out all my iniquities" probably refers to the fact that there was no sacrifice for murder and adultery in the Old Testament. David asks for mercy, that God would blot the sins out of His book.

Once the sins are blotted out, the joy which the sins took away needs to be restored. That is David's next request.

Restoring the Joy (51:8, 12)

In verses 8 and 12 David prays that God will return to him the joy of salvation he has enjoyed before. David isn't asking for God to restore his salvation but the joy of his salvation. David's salvation wasn't lost when he sinned, nor is ours. What was lost was the joy and refreshment of soul which salvation brings, which definitely will be lost when we try to hide our sin from God. We can think of the time David danced for sheer joy before the Lord as the ark of the covenant was transported up to Mount Zion in Jerusalem (2 Samuel 6:14). We do not get the impression from Scripture that David was a moody, downcast individual. From the many songs (psalms) he wrote and the enthusiasm with which he lived life, we can suspect that he took great joy in his relationship with God. But that joy had disappeared like the morning mist as a result of his concealed sin. And now he wants that joy back. He is tired of having his vitality drained daily like pond water in a time of drought. He wants to be filled afresh with the joy of salvation.

You probably know the feeling David had. No matter what the sin, joy is lost when sin is not confessed. A Christian with unconfessed sin in his life will be far more miserable than a non-Christian. Why? Because the Christian knows what the joy of the Lord is like and knows what he is missing by not being in fellowship with God. A person who has never experienced the joy of salvation could not know what that is like.

When the joy of salvation is restored, fellowship can be renewed—both with God and with man.

Renewing the Fellowship (51:11)

When David prays not to be cast away from God's presence and for the continuing presence of the Holy Spirit, he is asking for the renewal of fellowship. He wants the chasm between God and himself to be bridged so there is once again oneness and unity. Perhaps David is remembering how the Spirit of God left King Saul (I Samuel 11:6). He does not want the same thing to happen to Him.

Then David begins to focus on the future. In verse 12 he prays to be upheld by God's Spirit. Never again does he want to fail like he failed with Bathsheba and Uriah. Never again does he want to fail himself in delaying the confession of his sin for so long. Perhaps you have experienced something similar to what David went through. Once you have confessed your sin and been restored to fellowship with God, you feel the need to make some new covenants with God, to drive a stake in the ground, and to purpose never to traverse the same territory again. You ask the Lord for new strength and power to resist temptation and sin. You ask for a fresh filling of His Spirit in order to be upheld in strength in the future. When we have been cleansed of sin and its guilt and shame, that is exactly what we should do.

David's experience at this time in the whole process of his

restoration is best summarized in Psalm 32:1-2: "Blessed is he whose transgression is forgiven, Whose sin is covered. Blessed is the man to whom the Lord does not impute iniquity, And in whose spirit there is no deceit." "Blessed" means "happy," or "contented." Happy, satisfied, and content is the man whose sin is forgiven by God and who is restored to fellowship with Him.

Studying about David's sin may have raised unpleasant memories in your own mind of past sins in your life. I hope you have been through the same process David went through. No matter what sin any Christian has committed, no matter what condemnation you may have felt, or what guilt and shame you may have experienced, blessed contentment can only come through confession, forgiveness, and restoration. Don't ever think you have sinned too greatly for God to forgive you. You see that He forgave the double sins of adultery and murder that David committed. And He will forgive your sins as well.

But you must come as David came: accepting responsibility, acknowledging the sinfulness of sin, and addressing your confession to God. If you do that, you will enjoy all that David did. Your sin will be removed, your joy restored, and your fellowship renewed. The giant of guilt will be defeated.

APPLICATION

1. Read Ezra 9:1-10:17.
   a. What was the sin committed by members of the returning Jewish exiles? (verses 9:1-2)

   b. What was the response of Ezra the priest? (verses 9:3-4)

   c. Was Ezra himself guilty of the sin that was described?

   d. Why did he take on the responsibility of confession before God? (verses 9:5 ff.)

   e. Outline the content of Ezra's prayer of confession (the spirit as well as the content of his prayer) made in behalf of the people:

   (1) Verses 9:6-7

   (2) Verses 9:8-9

   (3) Verses 9:10-12

   (4) Verses 9:13-15

   f. How many times did he use the word "guilt" or "guilty" in his prayer?

   g. Describe Ezra's body language as he prayed (verse 10:1).

   h. What was the effect of his prayer of confession on those who were observing? (verse 10:1b)

i. What did the people who had sinned agree to do as a result of Ezra's confession in their behalf? (verses 10:2-4)

j. How do you know that Ezra's prayer was not purely ceremonial or perfunctory, that he was genuinely grieved over the sin of his people? (verse 10:6)

k. When Ezra gathered all the people together to set matters straight with God, what did he tell them they needed to do? (verse 10:10-11)

l. Describe how and why confession and repentance (a correcting of sinful behavior) go hand in hand.

m. Correcting national sins of this magnitude was a large undertaking. How can you tell that Ezra, as well as the people, were serious about making things right? (verses 10:16-17)

2. Read Nehemiah 1:1-11.
   a. How would you compare the distress Israel as a nation was in to the stress David was in when his own sin went unconfessed?

   b. Why was Israel suffering as a nation? (verse 7)

   c. What did Nehemiah do in order to restore fellowship between God and Israel? (verse 6b)

   d. How would you compare Nehemiah's request in verses 8-9 to David's request to have the joy of his salvation restored?

   e. How do we know that God accepted Nehemiah's prayer of confession for forgiveness and restoration of Israel? (compare verse 11b with 2:8b)

3. Read 1 John 1:8-10.

a. What is happening to us if we claim we have not sinned? (verse 8)

b. What will God do if we confess our sin to Him? (verse 9)

c. How does our concealing of sin reflect on God's character? (verse 10)

DID YOU KNOW?

The word "confess" comes from the Greek word *homologeo*. This word is made up of two words, *homo* (the same as) and *lego* (to speak). Therefore, *homologeo* means to say the same thing as or to be of one mind. When the Christian confesses, it is important that what is said is the "same thing as" what God says. That is, if we call adultery an "affair," or stealing "borrowing," or lust "an impulse," we have not called it the same thing God calls it and have not confessed our sins. Since all sin is sin against God, it is by His standards alone that our sin is judged. Make sure when you confess your sin that you are saying what God is listening for.

FACING THE GIANT OF TEMPTATION

I Corinthians 10:12-14

In this lesson we learn how to overcome the temptation to sin.

OUTLINE

There is at least one thing that is common to every human being who has lived regardless of race, age, or culture: temptation. Unfortunately, victory over temptation is far less universal. There is a key to unlocking the secret of victory—a key called the "way of escape."

   I.   **The Common Experience of Temptation**

  II.   **The Controlled Environment of Temptation**

 III.   **The Certain Escape from Temptation**
       A. Recognize the Possibility of Temptation
       B. Request Help in Advance of Temptation
       C. Resist the Devil and He will Flee from You
       D. Retreat from Certain Kinds of Temptation
       E. Remove any Means of Sin Far from You
       F. Replace Bad Influences with Good Ones
       G. Resolve to Live on the High Road

I   t was the 19th century Irish wit Oscar Wilde who confessed
    what many have thought over the years: "I can resist anything
    but temptation." No one can resist smiling knowingly not only
at the irony in that statement—but also at the reality of it. Temptation
is an ever-present factor in the life of every human being. From our
forebears Adam and Eve down to the present day, the failure to resist
temptation has been the source of countless tears of regret. The giant
of temptation has captured the lives of many people. We must learn
to defeat temptation if we are to walk victoriously in the spiritual
life.

Fortunately, God has provided a way of escape from the giant of
temptation. The apostle Paul wrote about that way in the passage of
Scripture we will study in this lesson, I Corinthians 10:12-14. I don't
know with certainty why Paul penned these specific words to the
Christians living in Corinth, but it must have had something to do
with the rampant wickedness in that city. Corinth was a seaport, a
crossroads in the Mediterranean world and, as such, was home to
every vice known to man. Paul may have written this particular part
of his first letter to the church at Corinth to help them defeat the
giant of temptation in their own lives.

That reasoning makes his words particularly applicable to us
today. We live in a society not unlike Corinth. Every conceivable
temptation flaunts itself daily in our culture, and far too many
Christians have become statistics in the war against sin. We need
Paul's words about escaping temptation as desperately as did the
Corinthian believers.

Paul starts by helping us understand the commonality of
temptation. No one is free from temptation, which means we must
face it as a constant foe, no matter who we are.

THE COMMON EXPERIENCE OF TEMPTATION (10:13A)

Paul begins by saying that no Christian experiences a unique
temptation; all temptation is common to man. Somehow we get the
idea that the temptations we face are unique; that no one else has
ever faced the particular kind of pressure we feel. That is not true,
Paul says. Temptation is the common enemy of every person on
earth. There are no unique situations which would excuse us from
the requirement to resist temptation and defeat it.

Scripture illustrates this truth from Genesis to Revelation. Abraham lied about his wife. Noah became intoxicated. David committed murder and adultery. Jonah rebelled against God. Peter denied the Lord Jesus. John Mark gave up on his missionary commitment. Paul and Barnabas became cross with one another. And even the Lord Jesus Himself was tempted—just as we are. The important thing to remember from Jesus' temptation is that temptation is not sin. Though He was tempted, He was also without sin (Hebrews 4:15).

Temptation is exposure to the possibility of doing the wrong thing. Such exposure is not sin; it is not the same as doing the wrong thing, which is sin. The Bible offers no hope that temptation is going to go away, but it does offer hope for resisting temptation. In fact, the longer we walk with the Lord and grow in maturity, the more intense and subtle the temptations seem to become. Satan seems to work overtime in devising traps and devices by which we might fall. We will not kill the giant of temptation this side of heaven, but we can defeat him.

Kenneth Taylor, who wrote *The Living Bible*, paraphrased verse 13 like this: "Remember this: the wrong desires that come into your life aren't anything new and different. Many others have faced exactly the same problems before you." So remember that temptation is common to you, to me, and to every believer. It is to be expected, so let's prepare for it and plan for its defeat.

THE CONTROLLED ENVIRONMENT OF TEMPTATION (10:13B)

One of the greatest truths about temptation is found in the last part of verse 13. If every believer in Christ could internalize this truth our battles with temptation would result in far more victories: Temptation occurs in an environment controlled by God, That is, the temptations God allows you to experience are not more than you can resist. You do not have to give in and sin.

God knows what our strength is, what our limitations are. Whenever I hear someone say, "It was more than I could handle," I know that is not true. Because the Word of God says all temptation is under God's control and He does not give us more than we can resist with His help. A good example of this in Paul's life is the experience he described in II Corinthians 1:8-10. He described himself as being tested beyond his own strength, and yet not beyond God's ability to deliver him. That is the core truth of Scripture regarding temptation as stated in verse 13.

Most people would prefer that life be free of temptations. But here is what would happen if that were true: You would never be able to demonstrate your great love for the Lord Jesus Christ. You would be kept from showing your loyalty to Almighty God and His holy principles as opposed to the things of the world. If we were simply automatons who were programmed to know God and to love God, God would receive no glory from our decisions to resist temptation and obey Him instead. When we resist temptation, God is glorified in our choices. Even though He gives us aid through the power of His Spirit, to resist or not is still our choice. And He is either glorified or not, depending on our choice.

THE CERTAIN ESCAPE FROM TEMPTATION (10:13c)

When we are tempted, God sees the end of the temptation (our escape) at the same time He sees the beginning of the temptation. When the test begins, God knows the way out. He doesn't figure it out as we go along. Because Christ Himself was tempted, "He is able to aid those who are tempted" (Hebrews 2:18). He is able to come to our aid immediately when we are tempted because He has already "been there and done that." He knows the way of escape and has it ready for us.

One of the things I have been learning as I get older is that temptation is not so much a matter of what we don't do as much as a matter of who we love. When we come to know the Lord Jesus, and we cultivate within our hearts a relationship of intimacy with Him, that in itself will keep us from many faults and many sins. His heroic image as the One who knew no sin becomes a powerful beacon for us. His ways of escape become ours through the indwelling of His Spirit. When we are living in fellowship with Him daily, it is hard to consider grieving Him, our Lord and best friend, by giving in to temptation. He becomes more than a preacher of do's and don't's—He becomes the way of escape who is always with us.

One further admonition born of experience: With every temptation we ever face there is a point when we know the way of escape is before us. If we choose not to take it, it will not be there later. There is "a way" (singular) of escape. We must take it when God shows it to us. Not to take it is an indication that we didn't want to escape to begin with, which raises another level of concern about our desire to obey God in the first place.

The word "escape" which Paul uses was sometimes used in Greek to describe a very narrow passage through which one passed—like the steep walls of a canyon which defined a very narrow passage through a rugged bit of terrain. The way of escape is like that. It is a single, narrow choice which must be made. There are not alternate ways out of that canyon of temptation. If we are going to get out, we have to take the one path that is provided. To turn and go a different way means being stuck in that place of temptation with no other escape.

Here are seven practical suggestions which I have found will help you choose the way of escape God provides and defeat the giant of temptation.

Recognize the Possibility of Temptation

The first indication that a person is setting himself up for a fall into sin is when he thinks he is beyond temptation. In verse 12, Paul states the case clearly: "Therefore let him who thinks he stands take heed lest he fall." The person who says, "That could never happen to me," is the most likely candidate to sin. "Pride goeth before destruction," says the King James Version (Proverbs 16:18).

A seminary professor who is a friend of mine kept track of ministers and students who failed in the ministry due to sexual temptation. When his list reached more than 100 names, he suddenly realized the common element. In all but two cases, he said, those on the list had been characterized by pride. Woe to the person who pridefully believes he is immune from any temptation.

Request Help in Advance of Temptation

Twice our Lord taught His disciples about the power of prayer as a defense against temptation (Matthew 6:13a; 26:41). Our daily prayer should be that God would protect us that day from the temptations which might enter our path. We should ask Him to make us sensitive, discerning, and aware of the very subtle traps the enemy might set. No soldier enters battle and then stops to sharpen his sword. Likewise, the best preparation for spiritual conflict is accomplished before the battle begins.

Resist the Devil and He Will Flee from You

James says that if we resist the devil he will flee from us. But the prior condition for that resistance is our submission to God (James 4:7). A key factor in resisting the devil is to submit to the Word of God as Jesus did in resisting Satan's temptations in the wilderness (Matthew 4:1-11; Luke 4:1-14). At the end of that period, when Jesus relied on verses from Deuteronomy to resist the devil's advances, the Bible says the devil "departed from Him." He will also depart from any believer who submits to the Word of God in resisting temptation.

Retreat from Certain Kinds of Temptation

Resisting temptation is always our responsibility, but how we do that can vary. One of the ways Scripture admonishes us to do that is to retreat—run from temptation. There are three kinds of temptation from which we should retreat quickly.

1. We are to retreat from idolatry

   We are to flee from idolatry (I Corinthians 10:14). An idol is anything that gets between you and God. While our idols may not be figurines sitting on a shelf in our home, there are certainly plenty of things which we are inclined to "worship" if given the opportunity. Flee from those things.

2. We are to retreat from immorality

   Twice the New Testament commands us to flee from immorality (I Corinthians 6:18; 2 Timothy 2:22). This is the most dangerous area of temptation because of the power of sexual attraction. It is a deception to think we can toy around with temptation in this area and come out unscathed. We are to imitate Joseph in the Old Testament who literally ran out of his master's house when he was being tempted by his master's wife—leaving his coat in her hands! (Genesis 39)

3. We are to retreat from greed

   First Timothy 6:10-11 says we are to flee greed. The pursuit of material things, the never-ending temptation to seek more, more, more, is what Paul warns against in this passage. Material things can become idols which come between us and God. The lure for mammon is so strong that Paul says to flee from it.

Remove Any Means of Sin Far from You

We have a responsibility not to make ourselves available to temptation. One man who was trying to lose weight decided he would only stop at the bakery if God provided a parking place directly in front of the store. A space became available on his eighth trip around the block. That's not exactly demonstrating a high level of commitment to resisting temptation, is it? Yet how often do we find ourselves creating similar scenarios as we toy with temptation?

Romans 13:14 says to "make no provision for the flesh, to fulfill its lusts" (Romans 13:14). Instead of setting ourselves up for failure we should set ourselves up for victory. Don't put yourself in a position where it's impossible not to sin. Put yourself in a place where it's not possible to sin by removing the means of sin far from you.

Replace Bad Influences with Good Ones

Proverbs 13:20 says, "He who walks with wise men will be wise, but the companion of fools will be destroyed." There is a definite tension involved in our lives as believers. On one hand we want to spend our time around godly people who will influence us and move us in the direction of maturity in Christ. On the other hand, if Christians are the only people we spend time with, how will non-Christians be won to Christ? The records of history are replete with multitudes of cases of well-meaning Christians being diverted from their standards of holiness in Christ by temptations encountered in their relationships with non-Christians. We must maintain accountability with other believers who can help us monitor our relationships. Who is having the most influence? Am I influencing this person for Christ or is this person influencing me toward the world and sin?

It is obviously the right thing to do to reach out to those who don't know Christ, or even Christians who are less mature and still struggling to overcome the world. But if you become trapped in a web of deceit and sin because of your involvement, it needs to stop until you can regain perspective and maintain accountability for your own life and standards in Christ. You need to replace bad influences with good ones.

Resolve to Live on the High Road

If you are a Christian already you need to resolve to get off the low road of commitment and live permanently on the high road. The high road is not free of temptation or spiritual pitfalls. But it is the road by which you are committed to taking the way of escape God provides in times of testing. You will be tested, and there will be a way of escape provided. But only those on the high road will see it and take it.

Why not decide today to be a Christian committed to defeating the giant of temptation. God has promised a way out of every test, but it still requires a choice from you in every instance. Chose the way God provides, and the giant of temptation will flee. That's a promise from God Himself.

APPLICATION

1. Read Proverbs 4:14-15.
   a. What is the central theme of these two verses?

   b. Whose responsibility is addressed here? Those who establish wicked paths or those who are contemplating whether to walk on them?

   c. Name five "paths" in our contemporary culture which many Christians are tempted to walk down but which can lead to downfall if taken:

   (1)

   (2)

   (3)

   (4)

   (5)

   d. What experience have you had with taking such a path?

   e. Why were you enticed to go down it? Did it appear harmless at first?

   f. How far down it did you go before you realized where it was leading?

   g. How did you get off that path?

h. What advice would you give to others as a warning about that path?

2. Read Proverbs 5:1-23.
   a. What value is there in listening to counsel about temptation? (verses 1-2)

   b. What do the metaphors in verse 3 suggest about the nature of temptation?

   c. What is the reality of temptation in spite of its appealing appearance? (verses 4-6)

   d. What principle for avoiding temptation is found in verse 8?

   e. What regret is voiced by those who failed to take the way of escape? (verses 11-14)

   f. What principle for avoiding sexual temptation is found in verses 15-20?

   g. By what is the one who fails led astray? (verse 23)

3. Read Proverbs 4:20-27.
   This passage is filled with excellent principles for defeating the giant of temptation. List those found in the following verses:

   a. Verses 20-22:

   b. Verse 23:

   c. Verse 24:

   d. Verse 25:

e. Verse 26:

f. Verse 27:

4. Read Matthew 4:1-11
   a. List the three temptations set before Jesus by Satan and the three
   Biblical responses (cite the Old Testament reference) with which
   Jesus defeated each temptation:

   Satan's Temptation   Jesus' Response
   (1)

   (2)

   (3)

b. Describe in your own words the importance of memorizing
Scripture as a tool with which to defeat temptation:

DID YOU KNOW?

S ubmarines which sink past a certain depth in the ocean will
be crushed by the intense water pressure. Yet there are soft
fish which swim freely at those depths without harm. How
can a ship ribbed with massive steel frameworks not withstand the
pressure, whereas seemingly vulnerable fish can? It is because fish
have a built-in method of equalizing the pressure. They can respond
to changes in water pressure, whereas humans cannot. Our goal as
Christians is not to fortify ourselves against the power of temptation.
Frankly, we are no match for the power of the flesh and the devil.
Rather, when we "equalize the pressure" through the presence of the
Holy Spirit, we are able to live in the midst of great pressure without
succumbing to it. He who is in us is greater than he who is in the
world (1 John 4:4).

FACING THE GIANT OF ANGER

Ephesians 4:25-32

In this lesson we learn to identify, and overcome, sinful anger.

OUTLINE

The Bible talks about two kinds of anger—one sinful, the other not. Why does God approve of any kind of anger? And which is which? Before setting out to defeat the giant of anger it would be wise to know the difference between the two.

I. **Recognizing Sinless Anger**

II. **Renouncing Sinful Anger**
  A. Don't Nurse Your Anger
  B. Don't Rehearse Your Anger
  C. Don't Converse About Your Anger
  D. Don't Cisperse Your Anger
  E. Do Reverse Your Anger

Early in the 1970's a promising young American pianist gave a concert in the chamber music room of the Erewan Hotel in Bangkok. A few moments into his opening piece he discovered that a certain key on the piano—one critical to the piece he was playing—was sticking. In addition, the piano stool had been oiled so excessively that he was constantly spinning around and facing the audience. Without stopping his first piece, he transitioned to his next number only to discover that another key began to stick. To try to loosen the keys he began kicking on the bottom side of the piano which caused one of the legs to give way, slanting the piano toward the floor. Too frustrated to continue playing, he marched off stage and reappeared with an ax with which he began to chop the piano to pieces. He stopped only when restrained by police.

It is safe to say that what the audience witnessed that night was a full-blown temper tantrum—anger in full bloom. Anger is among the most frequently cited spiritual giants we see stalking about in modern culture. And it seems its expression is on the rise. Today we have people shooting each other on the freeway in America over incidents that ten years ago would have just produced an expletive or two. People feel no hesitancy today in taking out their rage against another person in ways that end up sending them to jail or prison. Anger for many people is an uncontrollable emotion.

Ironically, anger can often do more harm to the person who expresses it than to the person who is on the receiving end of it. Someone has said, "Anger is an acid that can do more harm to the vessel in which it is stored than to the person on whom it is poured." Therefore, there are two reasons to learn how to defeat the giant of anger: to protect both the person who is angry as well as the person toward whom anger is directed.

Ephesians 4:25-32 is a key passage in Paul's epistles that will help us identify, and defeat, the giant of anger.

RECOGNIZING SINLESS ANGER (4:26A)

Paul says something in verse 26 which will surprise many Christians: "Be angry, and do not sin." The implication is, of course, that there is an anger which is not sin. It is possible to be angry without sinning. Anger has such a negative connotation that many people assume it is always sinful to be angry.

Before we clarify what Paul is saying, let's make sure we understand this: Paul is not giving permission here for the venting of frustration and rage. That is not the permissible anger he is talking about. Getting one's anger out is a popular theme in pop psychology today, but it has no Biblical basis. For instance, in *The Message,* Jesus' words in Matthew 5:22 are rendered this way: "I'm telling you that anyone who is so much as angry with a brother or sister is guilty of murder." Paul says anger is a work of the flesh (Galatians 5:19-21), and Proverbs says it is a fool who vents all his feelings (Proverbs 29:11). I have even read where secular thinkers are reconsidering the idea that venting anger is helpful. Studies indicate that venting one's rage only makes one angrier and solidifies those negative emotions.

So what is Paul referring to when he says to be angry, but do not sin? The answer is found in the life of the Lord Jesus Christ. There was more than one occasion on which He expressed anger, yet we know that He lived without sin. Therefore He wasn't manifesting self-centered rage or hostile venom toward others. Whatever He was doing, He was being angry without sinning.

The clearest expression of Jesus' anger is recorded in John 2:14-15 when He drove the merchants and money-changers out of the temple in Jerusalem. To understand why Jesus did what He did, we have to understand what was happening in the temple. The money changers and merchants were extortionists, cheating poor pilgrims out of their money. When Israelites came to the temple to offer a sacrifice, the animals they brought would be disapproved by the temple officials. They would be forced to purchase "approved" animals at an inflated price from the corrupt merchants and money changers. Jesus' anger was first directed at the injustice toward temple worshippers.

The second reason Jesus was so angry was because worship of God was being obstructed by the booths and tables set up in the Court of the Gentiles. This area of the temple was for Gentiles to come who wanted to worship the true God. They couldn't get near because the Court of the Gentiles had been turned into a mall of animal sellers and money changers.

How was Jesus' anger different from ours? His anger was never about His own "stuff"—His own agenda, His own schedule, His own rights, His own preferences, His own desires. That's what our anger is almost always about. His anger was over injustice and unrighteousness as manifested in the temple of Israel. That is the sort of righteous anger that is acceptable to God and that is not sinful. It would not hurt for Christians to express more of that kind of righteous anger toward the injustices in our world today.

On another occasion Jesus became angry at a group of people in a synagogue because they resented Him healing someone on the Sabbath (Mark 3:5). They were more concerned about the letter of the Law than they were about the spirit of the Law. They were more concerned with perfection than they were with compassion.

There is an anger that is righteous and not sinful. But it is always directed at the abuse of righteousness and justice and love and compassion. It is not used as a tool of retribution when we don't get our own way.

RENOUNCING SINFUL ANGER (4:26B)

In the same text there is also a kind of anger that is sinful—an anger which is not to be nurtured or condoned lest the devil see an opportunity to arouse bitterness and resentment in our lives. That kind of anger, Paul says later in verse 31, is to be put away from the believer's life. Sinful anger is by far the kind of anger that we are tempted to express most often. Here are some ways to avoid being defeated by the giant of sinful anger.

Don't Nurse Your Anger

When Paul says not to let the sun go down on our anger, he is saying, "Don't nurse your anger." Don't protect it and coddle it, giving it an ongoing place to live in your life. Be done with it in short order. While sundown is used here as a figure of speech, it is an excellent way to assess the state of your anger. If there is something you've been angry about during the day, make sure you put an end to it by the end of the day. Don't sleep on your anger—especially if your anger has been directed toward your spouse.

When we choose not to get rid of our anger, the danger is that it will become something worse than anger. Anger turns into resentment, and resentment turns into bitterness, and bitterness turns into unforgiveness, and unforgiveness turns into a defiled conscience. Pretty soon, we have become captives of our own anger. We can't think about anything except the person or issue which is the target of our anger. But if we release our anger by confessing it to the Lord and settling accounts if necessary with another person, we avoid the prison we were on the verge of creating for ourselves.

Let bedtime be a reminder: Am I nursing sinful anger toward anyone or anything?

Don't Rehearse Your Anger

Secondly, don't rehearse your anger. Some people love to tell others how angry they are. Henry Brandt used to say that when a person says to someone, "You make me so angry," they are saying something that isn't true. No one can make you angry. If you express sinful anger it is only because there is anger in you already. If another person does something that draws that anger out of you, the anger is not their fault—it's yours. If there was no anger in you to begin with, they could do the same thing and it would produce no sinful response in you at all. No one can cause us to become something which we are not.

When we verbalize our anger to another person all we are doing is confirming it, making our convictions deeper: "Yes, I am angry. That person has hurt me. The more I say it, the more I know I'm right." Verbalizing our anger just makes the roots of that anger go deeper and deeper into our heart. And the deeper the roots go, the harder it is to dig that anger out when you finally do realize you need to stop it. Don't make anger a part of your conversation. Like an actor, the more you rehearse the part, the more natural it becomes for you to play it.

Don't Converse about Your Anger

This is almost the same as not rehearsing your anger. While rehearsing your anger is done for the purpose of convincing and justifying yourself, conversing about your anger to others takes the form of corrupt communication coming out of your mouth (verse 29).

In the New Testament, the word "corrupt" was the word for "cutting." Paul is saying don't let words which have a cutting effect come out of your mouth. Americans have almost made a sport out of sarcastic, cynical, cutting forms of speech. Because it is so prevalent in our culture, it is easy to pick it up without even realizing it. That is not to blame the culture. We Christians are to blame for not practicing and obeying the Word of God. I believe Christians should purpose to remove sarcasm altogether from their vocabulary because of the danger of setting off a cycle of that kind of speech between two people once it is begun.

I recall learning a lesson about this kind of speech with a friend of mine. We would get together often for lunch, and good-naturedly rib each other, cut one another down, the way friends will often do. But suddenly my friend stopped being available for lunch; he would hardly acknowledge me when we were around one another. And so I went to him to find out what was wrong. It turns out something I had said in one of our sarcasm sessions had lodged in his heart and hurt him deeply. After we reconciled our relationship I purposed that I would never run the risk of damaging another person with "corrupt" cutting speech again.

Anger can fuel cutting communication. You can find yourself saying corrupt things about, or to, another person if you are harboring anger in your heart. Don't allow anger to fuel cutting conversation. The kind of speech we are to be characterized by is edifying speech, words that impart grace to the hearers (verse 29). Words that build up another person cannot be fueled by anger. Therefore we are to put anger aside.

One final point about conversation fueled or characterized by anger. If you associate with people who speak this way, you run the risk of speaking that way yourself (Proverbs 22:24-25). I don't like to be around angry people, and I hope you don't either on an ongoing basis. It's very difficult to be around that kind of person without becoming that kind of person yourself.

Don't Disperse Your Anger

Fourth, don't disperse your anger—nor your bitterness, wrath, clamor, evil speaking, or malice (verse 31). Sinful anger is just one of a number of sinful responses and behaviors that is not to proceed from the life of a Christian, a person controlled by the Holy Spirit.

To use modern language, I think Paul is talking here about a person who throws a temper tantrum when he can't get what he wants. Since my children are all grown, it's been many, many years since I've seen anything close to a tempter tantrum. But occasionally I will see one of my grandchildren have a fit just because he can't get what he wants, how he wants it, and when he wants it. Even if they were old enough to talk clearly they couldn't explain why they're so angry. They're just mad! And they're dispersing that anger onto everyone who happens to be around.

Anger is nothing more than a sophisticated version of a temper tantrum. Just because we can define it with eloquent speech doesn't mean it is any more justified. We are still mad that we can't get what we want. And our anger overflows out of us and defiles everyone around us.

Instead of nursing, rehearsing, conversing about, and dispersing our anger, we need to reverse our anger before it hurts us and others.

Do Reverse Your Anger

How do you reverse anger? Paul says (verse 32) you do it with forgiveness and lovingkindness and tenderness. You go to the person towards whom you have directed your anger and you minister to that person.

Paul says in Romans 12:20-21, "If your enemy is hungry, feed him; If he is thirsty, give him a drink; For in so doing you will heap coals of fire on his head." What does it mean to heap coals of fire upon someone's head? This expression grew out of an Egyptian custom. When a person had done something wrong, in order for him to express his contrition and shame for what he had done, he would place a pan of hot coals on his head to express the burning shame within his heart. So Paul says when we do good to those who have done us evil, when we go to that person and we show them love and tenderness, we put coals of fire upon their heads. We in essence shame them because of what they have done to us. We reverse what they have done to us by doing good to them.

So how do you reverse your anger? How do you heap burning coals upon the head of a person towards whom you have been angry, and who may have in fact done something to hurt you? See if you can figure out some way to demonstrate love towards him. But note: The point is not to shame the person. That still has an element of self in it. The point is simply to love him. If shame arises it will do so on its own when sin comes face to face with pure love. We are to love others in the way that God in Christ has loved us.

Is there someone today at whom you are angry? Slay the giant. A tender action of forgiving love is a weapon the giant of anger cannot withstand.

APPLICATION

1. Read James 1:19-20.
   a. Why do you think James grouped listening, speaking, and anger together in the same admonition? (verse 19)

   b. What is the most common way people reveal their anger?

   c. What impact would being "swift to hear" have on the expression of anger?

   d. Practically speaking, how do you think you could begin to implement James' admonition in your own life?

   e. In verse 20, is James referring to righteous indignation or sinful anger?

   f. Why doesn't man's wrath accomplish God's righteous purposes?

   g. How does righteous indignation accomplish God's purposes?

   h. Say someone attacks you unrighteously, and you respond in anger. Why isn't this demonstrating the righteous anger or indignation of God?

   i. Give an example of a valid expression of righteous anger or righteous indignation.

   j. If righteous indignation is acceptable before God, and we live in a society where much unrighteousness abounds, why don't we see more demonstrations of righteous indignation by Christians?

   k. Describe why you have, or have not, displayed the righteous indignation of God over injustice or unrighteousness that has come to your attention:

2. Read Psalm 37:1-11.
   a. How can "fretting" lead to anger? (verse 1)

   b. Instead of fretting (becoming angry) over the actions of the
   wicked, what should you do? (verse 3)

   c. Verses 4-5 are familiar verses to many Christians. How is their
   original context (verses 1-5) somewhat different from how they are
   often used when taken out of context?

   d. What is the desire of the heart that we are supposedly longing
   for? (verse 6)

   e. If you find yourself becoming angry over deeds committed
   against you, what are you to do? (verse 8)

   f. How does the context of verse 11 give no meaning to its familiar
   use by Jesus in Matthew 5:5?

   g. Instead of "weak" or "mild-mannered," how should the meek
   be thought of?

   h. In light of the context of Psalm 37:1-11, why do you think
   Jesus says the meek (those who refrain from becoming angry at
   evildoers) will inherit the earth?

3. What has been your personal experience with the truth contained
   in Proverbs 15:1?

   a. How would you compare a soft answer to the concept of heaping
   coals upon the head of your enemy?

   b. How successful are you at "holding your tongue" and delivering
   a soft instead of harsh answer?

c. How have you seen the truth of this verse bear fruit in your own life and relationships?

4. How have you witnessed, in your own life or in others' lives, the truth of Proverbs 22:24-25?

The verses are primarily a warning to avoid being influenced by angry people. a. Turning the verses around, how do these verses become a warning to the angry person? b. What negative influence could an angry parent have on his or her child(ren)?

DID YOU KNOW?

Anger is self-generated. James' famous words—be "slow to wrath" (James 1:19)—come right after his teaching on the origin of sin (James 1:13-15). In between the two passages he warns Christians not be deceived (James 1:16). That is, it's easy to be deceived into thinking that our anger is someone else's fault. But according to James, sin comes from our own evil desires. Evil desires conceive and give birth to sin, and sin leads to death—spiritual and emotional death that kills relationships. *Therefore,* James says, "be . . . slow to wrath," that is, watch for deception. The desire to be angry comes from inside ourselves. Giving in to that desire leads to ruin.

FACING THE GIANT OF RESENTMENT

Selected Scriptures

In this lesson we discover how to avoid the subtle dangers of resentment.

OUTLINE

Some sins in the spiritual life hit us head on and full force. Resentment is not like that. It is subtle, accumulating strength and momentum over time. But when it comes into its own, it can easily derail a mature believer. Resentment is a sin that needs to be stopped on day one.

   I. **The Examination of Resentment**

  II. **The Example of Resentment**

 III. **The Expense of Resentment**

 IV. **Five Steps to Defeating Resentment**
      A. Think It Through
      B. Write It Down
      C. Work It Out
      D. Talk It Over
      E. Give It Up

Americans have been shocked in recent years by incidents of random shooting in which innocent people have been killed or wounded. People are almost afraid to turn on the television or radio for fear of encountering another breaking news story of this kind. In almost all of these cases, those who know the perpetrator are in complete shock that the person would commit such a horrible act of violence. Often the person has no former criminal record, has raised no one's suspicions as far as being "on the edge" of violence, and appears to be a responsible citizen.

However, once an investigation begins into the background of a person who commits explosive acts of violence against others, it is not unusual for a pattern of seething resentments to emerge. Resentment bubbles and boils beneath the surface of a calm demeanor, ticking like a time bomb. The trouble is that no one, often not even the person himself, knows when the bomb will go off. Like the straw that breaks the camel's back, one final act which brings forth yet more resentment can set off violent acts.

Resentment may be among the most deceptive of the giants hiding in the forest of our lives. Unlike anger, which is more impulsive and sudden, resentment builds slowly and gradually over time. No one feeling of resentment is enough to trigger dangerous behavior, but add feelings of resentment up over time, and you have a volatile situation. And because resentment can be masked by an outwardly calm exterior, often it goes undetected by others. Accumulated resentment can lead in time to anger and bitterness— and yes, even to violence.

The giant of resentment needs to be banished immediately from our lives when it is first detected. Step one is to make sure we know what resentment is and how to detect its presence.

THE EXAMINATION OF RESENTMENT

We have to discover the meaning of resentment through the back door of the Greek language. The English word is not actually used in the New Testament, but the Greek word *logizomai* underlies what we refer to as resentment. An example of this is found in a negative context in the great love chapter of the Bible, I Corinthians 13. There Paul says that love "thinks no evil" (verse 5b).

Logizomai has its roots in the concept of bookkeeping. It means to calculate or to reckon. Entering a number into a ledger for the purpose of keeping track of it is what is meant by *logizomai*. The word is used to our benefit when it describes how God does not enter into His ledger a record of the sin of the person who is in Christ (Romans

4:8; II Corinthians 5:19). Paul also expressed hope that the failures of some in their actions toward him would not be recorded against them (II Timothy 4:16).

While there are many situations in which record keeping is essential, in personal relationships it is not only unnecessary but harmful. Love, Paul says, does not take into account wrongs that are suffered. Love doesn't write down and keep records of wrongs that are done. Love looks for a chance to erase the record of wrongs at every opportunity, to forgive and keep a clean slate.

THE EXAMPLE OF RESENTMENT

We find a sad example of resentment in the Old Testament Scriptures. When King David was dying, he brought Solomon, his son, before him and gave him some instructions. David still bore in his memory resentment over the actions of Joab, one of his military commanders. Joab had unlawfully killed two commanders in the army on the basis of his own resentments, and David had not forgotten it. David had remembered Joab's actions for years but had never avenged the deaths of his two commanders by killing Joab. So David called Solomon in and corrupted his mind by commanding that Joab not be allowed to die a natural death. In other words, David wanted Solomon to kill Joab (I Kings 2:5-6). David had nurtured his resentment for years and finally decided to act on it.

The trouble with resentment is that it is not static—it does not remain the same. Resentment is like a cancer that grows ever so slowly, eating away at the insides of the person who nurtures it. And, like cancer, ultimately other people become involved. Some people say, "If I want to be bitter and resentful that's my business." But, as Hebrews 12:15 points out, bitterness is a root that springs up and defiles many people in the process. Regardless of how benign you think your resentment is, it is not. Resentment is an evil root that is growing daily, waiting only for the opportunity to bring forth its fruit.

THE EXPENSE OF RESENTMENT

Experts agree that the one who nurtures resentment pays a high price to do so, both psychologically and physically. As I have mentioned earlier in these studies, doctors are documenting more and more instances in which anger, bitterness, and unforgiveness are the causative factors in physical diseases. S.I. McMillan, in his book *None of These Diseases* (Fleming H. Revell, 1963) says the estimates vary from 60 to 100 percent. Hypertension and heart disease are a major illness influenced by the stress brought about by unforgiveness.

Psychologically we are imprisoned by our past. We think we

have put another person under our control by our unwillingness to forgive, but it is really we who become the slaves of resentment. We become the embodiment of our resentment. Our life revolves around that which we refuse to let go of. Lewis Smedes, in his book *Forgive and Forget* (Pocket Books, 1984), tells a story which illustrates how a person's whole life can be bound up in his resentment. It is a story from a play based on World War II war crimes. A German officer was sentenced to prison for his part in wartime atrocities. Upon his release he and his wife planned to live out their life quietly in a cabin in the countryside.

A French journalist, whose entire family had been killed by orders of the German officer, had waited all the years the officer was in prison to extract vengeance. The court had not sentenced the officer to death, but the journalist had in his own heart. He stirred up resentment and hatred in a group of people who agreed to join him in putting the officer and his wife to death. On the afternoon of the planned killing, the journalist went to interview the officer and ended up revealing who he was, telling the German the story of his family. The journalist, upon meeting the aged officer, was suddenly softened by the man's difficult station in life and warned him that a mob was coming that night to kill him. He offered to lead the officer through the woods to safety.

The officer agreed to go on one condition: That the journalist forgive him—which he could not do. The journalist left and returned that night with the mob and killed the officer and his wife. He was willing to lead a person to safety whom he was not able to forgive. To forgive the officer would have meant giving up his whole reason for living. He had spent so many years focused on what the German officer had done to his family that to give that up would have meant giving up the purpose of his life.

Resentment exacts a high price from any who would choose to possess it. For those who want to live free from resentment, five steps are critical.

FIVE STEPS TO DEFEATING RESENTMENT
Think It Through

First, it is important to step back from the trees and try to get a picture of the whole forest. Just as we get so absorbed in reading a book or watching a movie or working on a hobby that we lose track of time, so we can lose track of the destructive nature of resentment. Do we really want to stay committed to something as destructive and harmful as resentment?

In all the research about resentment I have done, there seems to be one dominating reason for why people engage in it: Resentment gives people a feeling of superiority over the person toward whom their hate is directed. It makes them feel as if they are the righteous person who has been ill-treated by a lesser person. They enjoy fantasizing their plots of revenge. They mentally rehearse the story to themselves over and over, etching the details further into their memory with each retelling. Someone has said that resentment gives us two things: neurotic pleasure and religious pride.

Think it through! Is this what you are doing? Is it worth it to enjoy this sordid pleasure and risk your own health?

Write It Down

Write down why you are filled with resentment. I have discovered through counseling that often, when you ask a person consumed with resentment and unforgiveness to tell you why he is, he can't give a clear reason. Over time, the resentment has taken on a life of its own independent of what initially caused it.

If you will write down on a piece of paper in simple terms why you are resentful and read it out loud to yourself, it will sound totally different to you than it does when you rehearse it in your mind. Not only will it sound different; it won't have the emotion attached to it that you feel when you think about it. If you are honest it will sound far less justifiable, that is, there is something that happens to facts after being swirled around in the poison of resentment over time. They grow in size and seriousness. They get blown out of proportion. Reducing those facts back to their original size and shape by putting them on a plain piece of paper will help you regain perspective.

When you complete the following single sentence, "I am filled with resentment because . . .," do it when you're alone. Why? I predict that you will be a bit embarrassed when you discover that what is written on the paper is what you are so upset about.

Work It Out

A man who had been married for fifty years to the same woman was asked the secret of their marital bliss. "Well," he said, "it's kind of like this. When my wife and I got married, we made an agreement that whenever she was bothered about something she would just tell me off and get it out of her system. And if I ever got mad at her about something, I would take a walk. I guess you can attribute our marital success to the fact that I have largely led an outdoor life."

I'm not suggesting you can overpower anger with exercise. But there is a significant amount of research that suggests people who get regular physical exercise handle conflicts better than those who don't. Because most of us don't have jobs that are physically demanding, we have to create that situation artificially through exercise. Exhausting oneself with work or exercise seems to take an edge off of our emotions and helps to keep us "drained" of pent up feelings. It's not a cure-all (nor should it be interpreted as a recommendation to vent your rage on a punching bag), but exercise is as good for your soul as it is for your body.

Talk It Over

If you are a Christian, I know one of your friends—the Lord Jesus Christ. So I want to suggest to you that you talk over your resentments with Him in prayer. Perhaps you should read to Him what you wrote down on the piece of paper. Just tell Him, "Lord, here is why I feel resentful toward so-and-so." Then tell Him. You're not going to shock Him—He knows how you feel already. And it will begin a conversation that will hopefully lead to you resolving your resentment before it goes further and deeper.

I have read how missionaries learn to get leeches off their skin— by soaking in a warm bath of balsam. If they try to simply pull the leeches off, part of them will remain hooked in the skin and cause an infection. But in the warm bath they unhook themselves and can be pulled off cleanly. Bathing in the grace of God in the presence of Jesus has the same effect on resentment. It is hard to remain bitter and resentful while sitting in the presence of the Lord in prayer. Resentment will unhook itself from your heart and you'll find yourself able to lay it down. When you begin to ponder what the Lord has done for you, how He has forgiven your every sin and how he holds know resentments toward you when you sin against Him, you will begin to see the hypocrisy of holding resentments against others.

If you haven't accepted the forgiveness God offers for your own sins, it's much easier to hold on to your resentments toward others. But if you are a child of God who has been cleansed of sin against whom God holds no grudges, you should find yourself unable to maintain your resentment and unforginess toward others. We are to forgive others as God in Christ has forgiven us (Ephesians 4:32). And there is no better time to be reminded of that fact than when you are talking over your resentments with Him.

Give It Up

Clara Barton, founder of the American Red Cross, was once reminded of an especially cruel thing that someone had done to her years before—but she didn't seem to recall it. And her friend said, "Don't you remember?" Clara Barton said, "No, I distinctly remember forgetting it."

Did you know the only part of the Lord's prayer that is repeated is the part about forgiveness? "Forgive us our debts as we forgive our debtors," and clear at the end as an addendum to the prayer is this statement from Matthew that says, "For if you forgive men their trespasses, your heavenly Father will also forgive you. But if you do not forgive men their trespasses, neither will your Father forgive your trespasses" (Matthew 6:12, 14-15).

God's method for getting rid of resentments is through forgiveness. The Bible tells us that we are to love our enemies, bless those that curse us, do good to those that hate us, and pray for those that despitefully use us and persecute us. If we do this, it says, we will demonstrate that we are truly children of God. We are to act like our Heavenly Father. That's the only way I can explain some of the forgiveness I have heard about.

If you are nurturing some level of resentment toward a person or situation in your life, I urge you to work through the five steps above—and give it up. Your life free from the giant of resentment will be far sweeter and healthier in every respect.

APPLICATION

1. Read Matthew 18:21-22.
   a. How many times did Jesus tell Peter he needed to forgive his brother? (verse 22)

   b. What did Jesus mean by the particular number he mentioned (seventy-seven times)? (verse22)

   c. In light of Jesus' answer, should there ever be a time when a Christian bears resentment towards another person?

   d. Describe a time when you felt like you had forgiven someone as much as you were expected to. What makes a person think that resentment is somehow justified after a certain point?

   e. On the same basis, at what point in your life would God have been justified in beginning to resent your sins?

2. Read Matthew 18:23-35.
   a. What evidence of resentment did the king in Jesus' parable display? (verse 25)

   b. In spite of his obvious "sin," what did the servant ask for? (verse 26)

   c. Instead of resentment, what did the king offer in response to the servant? (verse 27)

   d. What resentment did the forgiven servant manifest toward his friend? (verse 28)

   e. How did the servant carry out his resentment? (verse 30)

f. What was the response of the king who had extended mercy to the servant? (verses 32-33)

g. Where did the resentful (unforgiving) servant end up? (verse 34)

h. Who does the king represent in the parable? (verse 35)

i. Who does the wicked servant represent?

j. Who does the fellow-servant represent?

k. Figuratively speaking, how does a person who bears resentment (unforgiveness) end up in jail? (verse 34)

l. How is he tortured? (verse 34)

m. What practical lessons about the dangers of resentment and the advisability of extending forgiveness can you draw from this parable?

3. Based on Ephesians 4:32 what right does a Christian have not to forgive others?

a. What three positive actions and attitudes should take the place of simmering resentment?

b. If there is anyone toward whom you bear some resentment, what kind, tender, or forgiving action or attitude could you manifest toward him or her this week?

4. Read Matthew 6:14-15. Complete the following sentences:
   a. If you forgive others God will . . .

   b. If you don't forgive others God will . . .

   c. Based on these words of Jesus, what point is there in asking God to forgive your sins if you bear resentment towards another person?

DID YOU KNOW?

I f you've ever watched the daredevils who climb sheer rock cliff faces you know how resentment works. These spider-like climbers can fit the tips of their fingers and toes around minute bumps and into sliver-sized cracks in order to inch their way up a cliff face. A tiny toehold is all it takes for them to make it to the next, more secure position. The apostle Paul says Satan is like that. All he needs is a foothold in order to gain access to a more secure place in our life. Just as something that doesn't look like a foothold is enough for a skilled climber to grab, so something that doesn't look like a serious sin is all the devil needs. Resentment is subtle, but it is still sin. The wise Christian will not do anything to give the devil a foothold in his life (Ephesians 4:27, NIV).

FACING THE GIANT OF DOUBT

John 20:24-29

In this lesson we learn how to turn doubt from a spiritual liability into an asset.

OUTLINE

In our world, doubt is a sign of weakness. "He who hesitates is lost," says the popular wisdom. But when doubt serves to confirm something previously believed, it becomes the greatest of strengths. Understanding and using doubt correctly is a step toward stronger faith.

I. **Facing the Giant of Doubt**
   A. Doubt Develops in Isolation
   B. Doubt Demands Evidence
   C. Doubt Draws Us Back to Christ
   D. Doubt Deepens Our Faith
   E. Doubt Defines Our Faith

II. **Fighting the Giant of Doubt**
   A. Admit Your Doubts Personally
   B. Articulate Your Doubts Clearly
   C. Acknowledge Your Doubts Prayerfully
   D. Analyze the Evidence Diligently
   E. Accept the Limitations Humbly
   F. Adjust to the Universe's Complexity

On February 15, 1947, an Avianca Airline flight bound for Quito, Ecuador, slammed into the side of 14,000 foot El Tablazo, a mountain peak not far from Bogota, Columbia. On that flight (there were no survivors) was a young New Yorker named Glenn Chambers. He was flying to Quito, Ecuador, to fulfill a life-long dream of becoming a missionary.

Before leaving the Miami airport earlier that day, Glenn had written a last note to mail to his mother. He had grabbed the only piece of paper he could find nearby, part of an advertisement that had the searching word WHY printed across the top. By the time his mother received that note in the mail, Glenn Chambers was dead. His mother asked "WHY?" concerning her son's death, as have countless others throughout history. Reconciling the "badness" of life with the goodness of God is only one of many reasons people sometimes have doubts.

The giant of doubt loves nothing better than a complex situation, such as the death of a missionary, to step in and tempt us to wonder if we're right about God after all. Doubts are not sin. But if doubts are not managed and handled appropriately they can lead to despair—or worse. In this lesson we study a situation in which a man named Thomas came face to face with the object of his own doubts. From his experience we can derive principles which will help us manage our own doubts, and do so in a way that will strengthen, not weaken our faith.

Doubt is not new in the spiritual experience of people who knew and trusted God. David and the other psalmists regularly cried out with uncertainty to God. Solomon wrote a whole book, Ecclesiastes, on what he considered the uncertainty of the reality we live in and around each day. And in the New Testament, John the Baptist was up front with his doubts, asking Jesus plainly, "Are You the Coming One, or do we look for another?" (Matthew 11:3) And this after he had baptized Jesus himself in the Jordan River—seeing the dove descend from heaven upon Him and hearing the Father proclaim that Jesus was His beloved Son (Matthew 3:16-17)!

The giant of doubt would love to move you from doubt to unbelief. But by applying the principles of this lesson you will learn to ask, and get answers for, those issues of faith which arise in every Christian's walk from time to time.

FACING THE GIANT OF DOUBT

John 20 records the story of the greatest doubter in the Bible, Thomas—a disciple of Jesus. From what I can gather about Thomas in Scripture, he appears to have been a melancholy sort—what we might call a pessimist today (John 11:16; 14:5). That's not altogether a bad trait. Melancholy people sometimes make good quality control experts because they're the first to spot the flaws or mistakes. They're always looking for proof. And being a doubter doesn't mean Thomas was an unbeliever. He apparently had been a faithful member of Jesus' band of twelve disciples. In fact, tradition suggests that it was Thomas who carried the Christian faith to India after the resurrection of Christ.

But it was the Resurrection that caused him to stumble. He had a hard time believing that Jesus was raised from the dead. Let's track Thomas' experience and see how his doubts were ultimately answered.

Doubt Develops in Isolation (20:24)

After the Resurrection, Jesus appeared to the disciples in a room where they had gathered. Apparently everyone was there except Thomas. We don't know why he was absent, but he was. Without speculating about what we don't know, let me set forth a principle that is true regardless of whether it was true of Thomas: Doubt flourishes in isolation. When you are separated from others who have strong faith, your faith can grow weaker. John the Baptist began to have his doubts about Jesus when he was isolated and alone in jail.

We can be isolated in more than a physical sense; we can also find ourselves isolated emotionally. I have found it to be profitable to take my emotional temperature whenever I find doubts coming into my mind. Sometimes if we are ill, or feeling discouraged, or we're separated from family and friends, doubts can find their way into our thinking much more easily. One of my favorite sayings is that "our souls and our bodies live so close together they catch each other's diseases." And C. S. Lewis, the brilliant British apologist, said he struggled seriously with doubts when he would be on a trip and find himself alone in a hotel room, separated from family and friends.

So be forewarned—isolation is a breeding ground for doubts.

Doubt Demands Evidence (20:25)

In verse 25, Thomas won't take the word of the other disciples concerning Jesus' resurrection. He demands proof. He wants to see the nail-prints in His hands and the spear wound in His side. It was Thomas who had warned the disciples about going to Jerusalem, fearing they would all be killed. And now that his fear has been realized, he finds it hard to believe that Jesus' death has been reversed—that He is alive.

The church has been hard on Thomas throughout history for his doubts. But I wonder if some of the other disciples actually didn't have as much faith as Thomas did. Thomas at least expressed his doubt and verbalized his desire for evidence. What may have seemed like faith in some of the others may have been a mask hiding their own doubts. We have to give Thomas credit for expressing his doubts and not being afraid of what he would find regardless of which way his investigation went.

We should never be afraid of wanting evidence. Granted, we may not always be able to get our hands on every piece of evidence we would like. But God is not afraid of our questions. And history has not yet revealed any evidence to contradict the Biblical record of Christianity. So don't be afraid of asking for evidence.

Doubt Draws Us Back to Christ (20:26)

Eight days after Jesus first appeared to the disciples, He came to them again. And this time Thomas was with them. Perhaps Thomas purposed to stick closer to the group than he had done at first so as not to miss Jesus if He appeared to them again.

In our quest for answers and evidence we ultimately must come in contact with a person—the Lord Jesus Christ. Christianity is not about doctrines and creeds. Christianity is about Christ. If we examine the right evidence, what we will find are not answers but Christ. That's what happened to Thomas. In his search for evidence, he found Christ.

Sometimes it is too easy to get completely wrapped in what we don't know, what we don't have answers for. In truth, the things we usually have questions about represent just a small minority, a tiny percentage, of the things revealed to us in Scripture about God and our faith in Him. And we get hung up on those things, majoring in minors. Someone has said we need to believe our beliefs and doubt our doubts. That's not bad advice. If we do that, we won't welcome with open arms every doubt we have as if it is automatically accurate and correct. We will, instead, view our doubts with a measure of caution, even skepticism. We'll hold them at arm's length until we're sure they represent something to pursue evidence for. In doing so, we hold the giant of doubt at bay, keeping him under our control.

Doubt Deepens Our Faith (20:27)

It's possible that Thomas never would have seen Jesus if he hadn't doubted. He might not have rejoined the disciples without the motivation of seeing for himself whether Jesus was alive. And because he doubted and pursued the evidence, he had an amazing testimony to share. He had touched Jesus' wounds with his own hands. He had first-hand knowledge that the Jesus who died on the cross was the same Jesus who had come back from the grave.

Honest doubts have the potential for building an indestructible faith if you will follow those doubts. Just as Jacob wrestled with the angel in Genesis (32:24) and came out of that experience a changed person, so your own doubts can cause you to come out stronger and more resilient in your faith. I have heard more than one person say that as they began to search for evidence they found something they weren't expecting—a deeper relationship with God. They say, "I don't even care about the answers any more. I've found the Lord in a whole new way."

Don't be surprised if you discover more than answers when you begin to confront your doubts about your faith.

Doubt Defines Our Faith (20:28)

Somebody has said that "There is more faith in one doubt than in half the creeds." What that means is that when we follow a doubt all the way through to the resolution of it in our heart, we can say with Thomas, "My Lord and my God." That is one of the greatest professions of faith in all of the Bible, and it came on the heels of one man's doubts. Thomas' faith was defined like never before when he followed his doubts to their conclusion.

Some people are so steeped in the facts of Christianity that their faith has grown cold. They sort of keep it in reserve, like canned vegetables stored up for winter eating. When a doubt comes they're forced to get their faith off the shelf and redefine it to make sure of what they believe. That is a positive thing when it happens.

FIGHTING THE GIANT OF DOUBT
Admit Your Doubts Personally

This is not always easy to do. You're probably not going to be inclined to go to prayer meeting and stand up and give testimony to your doubts—especially while everybody else is testifying to how great his or her walk with the Lord is going. But honesty is where it starts. You don't have to announce your doubts to the church, but you do need to verbalize them carefully to yourself. And perhaps even to a trusted friend or mentor in the faith, or your pastor. Separating what you're not sure about from what you are sure about is step number one.

Articulate Your Doubts Clearly

If you don't do this Satan will grab the opportunity to convince you that you're just a doubter who can't believe anything. That's not true. If you're a Christian you already believe a significant number of things with conviction. Be clear about the specific things you have questions about. Do you doubt the accuracy of the Bible? The reality of the Resurrection? The existence of heaven or hell? That there's only one way to God, through Christ?

And why do you doubt? Have you been influenced by a book? A professor? Another believer? A non-believer? Identifying your doubts and their source will help you understand what you need answers for and why.

Acknowledge Your Doubts Prayerfully

Here is the most important point I want to make about fighting the giant of doubt: You must turn your doubts into prayers to God. Think of the people in the Old Testament whom God greatly used who had doubts when they heard His plans for them—Sarah, Moses, Gideon, and Jeremiah just to name a few. These people were approached by God Himself and they still doubted! And God knew their doubts just as He knows yours and mine. We don't turn our doubts into prayers to God in order to inform God of our doubts. We tell God in order to verbalize what we are thinking and feeling about our faith. That makes it more understandable to us as we try to figure out what is going on in our lives.

Go to God with your doubts. He is waiting to hear from you.

Analyze the Evidence Diligently

It's one thing to sit back and entertain your doubts and wonder what the answers are. It's another thing to take responsibility for finding the answers and search diligently for them. Sure, it takes some effort to do so. But the answers are there for most of the questions we have about the faith. You and I are not the first persons to have had the doubt we are having ("There is nothing new under the sun." Ecclesiastes 1:9). Many brilliant Christian scholars have tackled the great questions of the faith and produced mountains of answers and evidence. If you don't know where to look, ask your pastor or visit a Christian bookstore. Part of the responsibility that goes along with having questions is being willing to seek out the answers.

Accept the Limitations Humbly

1. Accept your own limitations

   The more I study, the more I discover I don't know—and I study all the time! I continually pray that God would give me greater capacity to learn and know about Him. But I accept the fact that I will never know it all—and so should you. There are definite limitations to what we have the capacity and intelligence to know. So work as hard as you can, but accept your limitations.

2. Accept the Bible's limitations

Here is what I mean by this: Everything in the Bible is true, but not all truth is in the Bible. The Bible is not an encyclopedia or textbook containing the answer to every question in the world. That is not why it was given to us by God. But here is the most important thing to remember: The Bible has everything you need to know in order to know God and receive eternal life through faith in His Son. If you have other questions which are answered in the Bible, all the better. But if the Bible doesn't have the answers, don't doubt the answers the Bible does have.

Adjust to the Universe's Complexity

There is so much about the universe, and the God who made it, that we simply do not know. The bottom line is that we will never understand God and all of His ways. We are not supposed to. If we could, we would be like Him (and the last people that aspired to that goal got all of us in a lot of trouble; Genesis 3:5 ff.).

So we need to be reconciled to our place in the grand scheme of things. God's purposes, and what He has revealed to us of them, are moving ahead on His timetable. And He has told us what we need to know to make sure we are safely on board. As for what we don't know, use your doubts as assets, as tools to draw you closer to the truth. Put the giant of doubt in its place by solidifying your place in the faith.

APPLICATION

1. Read Exodus 3:10-15; 4:1-13.
   a. What was Moses' first expression of doubt concerning God's instructions to him? (verse 3:11)

   b. What was it he doubted?

   c. What was God's response to his doubt? (verse 3:12)

   d. What was Moses second expression of doubt? (verse 3:13)

   e. How did God respond? (verses 3:14-15)

   f. What was Moses third expression of doubt? (verse 4:1)

   g. How did God respond? (verses 4:2-9)

   h. What was Moses fourth expression of doubt? (verse 4:10)

   i. And God's response? (verses 4:11-12)

   j. How did Moses respond to all of God's answers? (verse 4:13)

   k. What does it imply when we get answers to all our questions but still don't want to believe or obey?

2. Read Judges 6:11-22, 36-40.
   a. What is Gideon's first expression of doubt about God's words? (verse 13)

   b. How did the Lord respond? (verse 14)

c. What is his second, more personal, expression of doubt? (verse 15)

d. What is God's answer? (verse 16)

e. Third, what kind of proof did Gideon ask for? (verses 17-18a)

f. How does the Lord respond? (verses 18b-22)

g. What is Gideon's fourth expression of need for certainty? (verse 36-37)

h. What answer did he get? (verse 38)

i. How does Gideon ask for his final display of evidence? (verse 39)

j. And how did God respond? (verse 40)

k. How did Gideon apparently respond after getting the evidence he needed? (verse 7:1)

l. How would you compare Gideon's final response to Moses?

3. What do you learn from the following Scriptures about the man's ability to gather 100 percent of the evidence about God and His ways?

a. Deuteronomy 29:29

b. Isaiah 55:8-9

c. Romans 11:33-34

4. What are the two or three biggest questions (doubts) about your faith that you wish you had immediate answers for?

a. Describe the degree of influence these questions have on your faith overall.

DID YOU KNOW?

I n all of life, we cross a line at some point that says, "I know enough. It's time to act." Whether it's building a house, having children, or taking a new job—we live with a tension between what we know and what we don't know. Here's the question to ask: Is what I know sufficient for me to move ahead and exercise faith about what I don't know? The apostle Paul said, ". . . we walk by faith, not by sight" (2 Corinthians 5:7). If we could see it all, we would not need faith. "Watch, stand fast in the faith, be brave, be strong. Let all that you do be done with love" (I Corinthians 16:13-14). "And, whatsoever you do, do it heartily, as to the Lord and not to men knowing that from the Lord you will receive the reward of the inheritance, for you serve the Lord Christ" (Colossians 3:23-24).

FACING THE GIANT OF PROCRASTINATION

Acts 24:22-27

In this lesson we discover the dangers of putting off until tomorrow what should be done today.

OUTLINE

Have you been given "a round Tuit," a small coin with the word "Tuit" engraved on it? It's for people who are always planning on getting "around to it." We joke about procrastination, but it is no laughing matter. The results could be eternally devastating

   I. **Procrastination Robs You of Opportunities for Service**

  II. **Procrastination Robs You of the Opportunity to Be Successful**

 III. **Procrastination Robs You of the Opportunity for Salvation**
   A. The Identity of the Procrastinator
   B. The Instruction of the Procrastinator
   C. The Impact on the Procrastinator
   D. The Intention of the Procrastinator

  IV. **Procrastination's Two Big Problems**
   A. Procrastination Produces a False Sense of Control
   B. Procrastination Ignores the Uniqueness of Conviction

Years ago, a very famous preacher surveyed the Bible to
discover the most important words in Scripture. For instance,
he wanted to find the saddest word in the Bible, the happiest
word, and the most emotional word—along with a long list of
additional words which were the superlatives in their category. When
he came to the most dangerous word in the Bible you might be
surprised to know what he chose: Tomorrow. That's right—tomorrow.
Tomorrow is the most dangerous word because of its ability to rob
dreamers of their dreams. It has robbed students of their educational
opportunities and fathers of their relationships with their children.
More than anything, it has kept more people from coming to Christ
and finding salvation than any other word in the dictionary.

Satan's favorite word is "tomorrow." If he can get someone to
keep putting off thinking about his salvation until tomorrow, he has
them right where he wants them. He uses tomorrow like the owner
of the gas station who put a sign up that said, "Free gas tomorrow."
Every time you look at the sign it puts you off one more day. "Today"
is the word that is dear to the heart of God, as in ". . . today is the day
to be saved!" (II Corinthians 6:2, Today's English Version).

In this lesson we're going to meet the giant of procrastination. It
was active in the life of a Roman official named Felix whose story
we find in Acts 24:22-27. Felix, and his wife Drusilla, missed the
opportunity for salvation because of procrastination. Through them
we will discover the dangers of procrastination and how to defeat it.

PROCRASTINATION ROBS YOU OF OPPORTUNITIES FOR SERVICE

Jesus was talking to some of His followers once about the cost
of discipleship. The essence of His words to them was that life has
a way of putting obstacles in the path of the one who would seek
first the Kingdom of God (Luke 9:59-62). Things such as taking
care of family and the requirements of vocation are legitimate
responsibilities. Was Jesus saying we should ignore those things in
order to follow Him?

Of course not. He was simply illustrating that it's always easy to
think of lots of reasons why we "can't" respond to the call of God in
our life. Once we take care of all those details, we think, then we'll
get serious about following Christ.

Matthew 26 relates one of the saddest stories in the New
Testament of a missed opportunity that could never be retrieved.
Jesus went into the Garden of Gethsemane on the night of His
betrayal and arrest. He took Peter, James, and John into the garden

with Him. Three times Jesus went aside to pray and three times discovered that His three friends had fallen asleep. They couldn't have known of the historical significance of what was happening at that moment. But we can be sure that later they would have given anything to replay the events of that night. They would have wanted to stay awake and watch and pray for their Lord in His hour of agony. But they let one of the most critical nights in history pass them by.

One day in heaven each of us will no doubt look back and realize critical moments and hours of decision which we let slip through our fingers because of procrastination. If you're like me, there are times when I sense the Lord's leading to reach out to a certain person. And then I get busy and fail to follow up on it, only to discover later that there was something difficult going on in that person's life. Because I put off the Lord's leading I missed the opportunity to reach out and minister to that person. That's an awful feeling to live with.

I have a feeling that after reading this lesson on procrastination the Lord will bring a person to mind—maybe more than one—that you have been meaning to call or reach out to. Respond to Him as soon as He speaks to your heart. I'd rather you obey Him than finish reading this chapter! Don't let anything stand in the way of following His leading in matters of spiritual urgency, whether in your life or the life of another person. Life is too precious and the consequences too eternal to do anything less than obey when we have the chance.

PROCRASTINATION ROBS YOU OF THE OPPORTUNITY TO BE SUCCESSFUL

No one who is a practicing procrastinator succeeds at anything. Procrastination robs you of the opportunity to succeed. Charles Swindoll describes the effect of procrastination as if procrastination were human. He personifies procrastination in a most effective way:

"Procrastination comes out a winner every time. . . . He can outtalk any student when it comes to homework. He can out think any executive when it comes to correspondence. He can outwork any homemaker when it comes to vacuuming or doing dishes. He can outlast any parent when it comes to discipline. He can outsmart any salesman when it comes to selling. He has one basic product and he centers all his energy toward that single goal: defeat! By the sheer genius of suggestion he becomes the epitome of what he destroys: success."

You see, if we cannot take action when it is thrust upon us, we are doomed to defeat and failure.

He was going to be all that a mortal should be
　　　　To-morrow.
No one would be better than he
　　　　To-morrow.
A friend who was troubled and weary he knew,
Who'd be glad of a lift and who needed it, too;
On him he would call and see what he could do
　　　　To-morrow.
Each morning he stacked up the letters he'd write
　　　　Tomorrow
And thought of the folks he would fill with delight
　　　　To-morrow.
It was too bad, indeed, he was busy to-day,
And hadn't a minute to stop on his way;
More time he would have to give others, he'd say,
　　　　To-morrow.
The greatest of workers this man would have been
　　　　Tomorrow.
The world would have known him had he ever seen
　　　　Tomorrow
But fact is he died and faded from view,
And all that was left when his living was through
Was a mountain of things he intended to do
　　　　Tomorrow.
[Edgar A. Guest, "Tomorrow," A Heap O'Livin',
Reilly and Lee Company (Chicago: 1916).]

Any businessman or salesman will tell you that the art of succeeding is knowing what to do and when to do it—and doing it at that moment. Thomas Huxley was not a spiritual man but he did have it right when it came to understanding procrastination: "The most important result of all education is to make you do the thing you have to do, when it ought to be done, whether you like it or not. It is the first lesson that ought to be learned. And however early a man's training begins, it is probably the last lesson that he learns thoroughly." What is that lesson? To do the thing you have to do when it has to be done.

Most people keep some sort of "To Do" list where they write down the tasks and goals they have for the day or week. But how many people purposefully take the hardest, most distasteful task and move it directly to the top of the list? Rather than pushing it to the bottom of the list, the person who is willing to do the hardest job when it needs to be done is on the road to success.

All of these practical reasons for defeating procrastination are important on a day-to-day basis. But there is another reason for conquering procrastination that is far more important. Procrastination can keep you out of heaven.

PROCRASTINATION ROBS YOU OF THE OPPORTUNITY FOR SALVATION

Procrastination can keep you from becoming a Christian. That's what happened to two people we meet in Acts 24, Felix and Drusilla.

The Identity of the Procrastinator (24:24a)

Some background on these two individuals will help you understand their spiritual situation:

1. Felix was Antonius Felix. Greek by birth, he gained his appointment as Roman Procurator of Judea from his brother.

2. Drusilla, Felix's wife, was one of three daughters of Herod Agrippa I. Felix induced her to leave her husband and marry him. Her father, Herod Agrippa I, was the one who murdered James, the brother of John, and tried to murder Peter as well (Acts 12). Her great-uncle, Herod Antipas, was the one who executed John the Baptist, and her great-grandfather, Herod the Great, was the one who ordered the murder of all the baby boys in Bethlehem in an attempt to eliminate Jesus. This was Drusilla's family heritage. Spiritually dark, to say the least.

The apostle Paul was brought before Felix on charges of sedition. When Paul spoke, it was not to defend himself but to proclaim the gospel of Christ. No matter where Paul went he always had one mission—to declare the gospel. When Paul began to speak, it was almost as if Felix had been brought before Paul instead of Paul having been brought before Felix.

The Instruction of the Procrastinator (24:24)

Paul spoke to Felix and Drusilla about his faith in Christ, and about three further points: ". . . righteousness, self-control, and the judgment to come." That sermon was well-suited to Paul's audience that day because Felix and Drusilla were definitely needy in all three areas. We've already established that they were unrighteous people. Their marriage was immoral and their backgrounds were filled with spiritual darkness. They no doubt felt quite uncomfortable at Paul's words.

Then Paul moved on to self-control, another foreign word to them. They were used to doing whatever they wanted, unencumbered by moral restraints of any kind. And then he concluded with the natural outcome of unrighteousness and lack of self-control—judgment. Paul told them there is a Judge sitting on a throne much larger than the throne of the Procurator of Judea; even the throne of the Emperor himself in Rome. Someday, Paul told them, they would stand before that Judge and He would call them to account for their sins. That must have been some sermon, one that Felix and Drusilla never imagined they would hear when they woke up that morning.

The Impact on the Procrastinator (24:25)

Felix's response to Paul's sermon was something we don't see much in contemporary preaching: fear. But "Felix was afraid" as a result of what he had heard from Paul—he was "terrified" in the words of the old American Standard translation. God had spoken mightily to Felix's heart, and he was overtaken by fear at the prospect of future judgment in light of his past and present life.

But then, at the very time when he could have had all of his fears relieved, Felix said that most dangerous of words (in a manner of speaking): "Tomorrow."

The Intention of the Procrastinator (24:25)

Felix sent Paul away, saying he would call for him again at a more convenient time. Felix procrastinated, didn't he? He put off life's most important, and sometimes most difficult task—getting right with the God who created, and who will judge, us all. We don't know if Felix ever believed the gospel of Christ or not. Given his initial response, we would say the likelihood was not good. Even if he did later, we do know that he passed up the first chance God gave him to be saved. He put off until a "convenient time" that which he should have grasped immediately. There is never a "convenient time" to be saved. The time to be saved is when God shows you your need. Who knows whether you will ever sense that need again?

PROCRASTINATION'S TWO BIG PROBLEMS

Procrastination is dangerous in any arena, but nowhere is it more dangerous than in the realm of salvation.

Procrastination Produces a False Sense of Control

First of all, procrastination gives us the impression that we are in control of tomorrow. It does not take into account the uncertainty of life. If we knew for certain that tomorrow would come, perhaps we could put off some things. But who knows what life holds past today, past this minute? No one (Proverbs 27:1).

Scripture uses eighteen different metaphors to remind us of the transitory nature of life. For instance, life is like a vapor, here one minute and gone the next. Who would try to build their future on a vapor? That would be a foolish prospect indeed. To assume we can put off until tomorrow that which we should do today is a prescription for remorse—possibly eternal remorse.

The very James who had missed the opportunity to watch and pray with Jesus in the Garden of Gethsemane apparently learned his lesson. In his letter to the churches, he warns about the presumption of thinking we are in control of tomorrow. Life is a "vapor that appears for a little time and then vanishes away" (James 4:14).

Are you putting off until tomorrow a decision about your own salvation? Or a decision to begin walking as a committed disciple of Christ, laying aside the things of this world and living only for Him? Perhaps you hear the gospel presented regularly in church or on the radio, and you keep telling yourself you need to respond and get things settled with God. If you are putting this off, you are building your future on a foundation of vapor. You do not know what tomorrow will bring. Today is the day for salvation.

But let's assume you have absolute control over tomorrow; that you know exactly how many days left you have to live. There is still a problem. You don't know whether conviction will ever touch your heart again.

Procrastination Ignores the Uniqueness of Conviction

I refer to the special times when God deals with each person as "defining moments." Every Christian can think back to the time he was saved and recognize the uniqueness of the situation. Something happened that day that had not happened the day before. The moment of your salvation was a unique event when God brought together all the factors and influences necessary in order to recognize your need for Him.

You may get a tomorrow, but there is no guarantee that when tomorrow comes you will be convicted of your need for Christ. Just as it happened with Felix—he came under sincere conviction the day Paul preached to him—it happens to each of us. The danger is that we, like Felix, will ignore that conviction and put it off until a more "convenient time." The problem is that the convenient time may never come. You may never be convicted again of your need for salvation.

The prophet Isaiah said it best: "Seek the Lord while He may be found, call upon Him while He is near" (Isaiah 55:6). If you know the Lord can be found today, then today is the day you need to call upon Him—while He is near.

Procrastination is a giant that will rob you of opportunities for service and the opportunity to be successful. But most of all it will rob you of the opportunity to be saved. Don't put off doing anything that you know needs to be done today. You have no guarantees about tomorrow and no promise that the promptings you feel today will ever be there again. Whatever you do, don't procrastinate about being saved. Today may be the only chance you have.

APPLICATION

1. Read Exodus 3:10-15; 4:1-13.
   a. What was Moses' first expression of doubt concerning God's instructions to him? (verse 3:11)

   b. What was it he doubted?

   c. What was God's response to his doubt? (verse 3:12)

   d. What was Moses second expression of doubt? (verse 3:13)

   e. How did God respond? (verses 3:14-15)

   f. What was Moses third expression of doubt? (verse 4:1)

   g. How did God respond? (verses 4:2-9)

   h. What was Moses fourth expression of doubt? (verse 4:10)

   i. And God's response? (verses 4:11-12)

   j. How did Moses respond to all of God's answers? (verse 4:13)

   k. What does it imply when we get answers to all our questions but still don't want to believe or obey?

2. Read Judges 6:11-22, 36-40.
   a. What is Gideon's first expression of doubt about God's words? (verse 13)

   b. How did the Lord respond? (verse 14)

c. What is his second, more personal, expression of doubt? (verse 15)

d. What is God's answer? (verse 16)

e. Third, what kind of proof did Gideon ask for? (verses 17-18a)

f. How does the Lord respond? (verses 18b-22)

g. What is Gideon's fourth expression of need for certainty? (verse 36-37)

h. What answer did he get? (verse 38)

i. How does Gideon ask for his final display of evidence? (verse 39)

j. And how did God respond? (verse 40)

k. How did Gideon apparently respond after getting the evidence he needed? (verse 7:1)

l. How would you compare Gideon's final response to Moses' response?

3. What do you learn from the following Scriptures about the man's ability to gather 100 percent of the evidence about God and His ways?

a. Deuteronomy 29:29

b. Isaiah 55:8-9

c. Romans 11:33-34

4. What are the two or three biggest questions (doubts) about your faith that you wish you had immediate answers for?

a. Describe the degree of influence these questions have on your faith overall.

DID YOU KNOW?

The Latin word for tomorrow was cras, from which the adjective, *crastinus,* "of tomorrow," was derived. The prefix *pro* meant "forward" or "toward." Therefore, the Latin verb *procrastinare* came to mean "put forward to tomorrow." The person who procrastinates is the person who promises himself each day, "I will do it tomorrow." And when tomorrow comes, the same promise is made again and again. That is, tomorrow is always 24 hours away. Tomorrow is close enough to keep us from feeling overly guilty, far enough away to avoid the discomfort we feel about getting it done at all. One wonders if Latin *cras* (tomorrow) was connected to *crassus,* the Latin word for "dense." Procrastinators could certainly be called crass as we define it today—"lacking in discrimination and sensibility."

FACING THE GIANT OF FAILURE

II Corinthians 4:7-18

In this lesson we learn how to succeed at the art of failure.

OUTLINE

Everyone can become an expert in at least one discipline in life if he so chooses: the discipline of turning failure into success. Learning God's perspective on failure only has one prerequisite: that we have failed at least once. Therefore, everyone qualifies!

I. **Facing the Giant of Failure**
   A. Facing the Reality of Failure
   B. Facing the Reason for Failure
   C. Facing the Result of Failure

II. **Fighting the Giant of Failure**
   A. Acknowledge Your Failure
   B. Accept God's Forgiveness
   C. Apply the Lessons of Failure Toward Success
   D. Accept Failure as a Fact of Life, Not a Way of Life
   E. Arise from Failure and Start Again
   F. Avoid Judging Failure in Others

I t's one thing when you and I have an experience of failure in
our private lives. Our failure is known only to a small circle of
friends and family. But it's a totally different thing when you're
the most important political leader in the world and your every move
is reported live by the news media around the world. Such was
the case when President George Bush became ill and vomited at a
state dinner in Japan—unfortunately including the Prime Minister of
Japan in the "effects" of his ill health.

Granted, that probably doesn't qualify as a personal failure.
We don't normally hold people responsible for illnesses they have
no control over. But try telling that to former President Bush. He
probably felt himself a failure when his embarrassing moment in
Japan took place. Indeed, when he had lain down on the carpet in
order to be attended to by his physician he moaned, "Just roll me
under the table until dinner is over." At least his "failure" didn't
cloud his sense of humor.

A bit better example of what we traditionally think of as failure
happened in 1957 when the Ford Motor Company released to the
public what it called "the car of the decade"—the Edsel. It was
supposed to be the most dramatic advance in engineering and
design since the invention of the automobile a half-century earlier.
Unfortunately, it turned out to be the biggest bomb in the history of
the automotive industry. It was, to put it mildly, a colossal failure.
Ford's best efforts to succeed turned out to be the worst effort in the
company's history.

Life is filled with failure, whether presidential, corporate, or
personal. The person who does not learn to manage failure, to
defeat the giant of failure, will soon find himself buried under a
mountain of disgrace and shame. But the person who learns to profit
from failure will find himself climbing ever higher mountains of
accomplishment. What the giant of failure means to trip you with can
turn out to be a ticket to the future. But only if we understand failure
from God's perspective.

FACING THE GIANT OF FAILURE

In 1988, the United Technologies Corporation published an ad in
The Wall Street Journal reminding us of our failures. The ad said,

> You've failed many times, although you may not remember.
> You fell down the first time you tried to walk.
> You almost drowned the first time you tried to swim.
> Did you hit the ball the first time you swung a bat?
> Heavy hitters, the ones who hit the most home runs,
>   also strike out a lot.

R. H. Macy failed seven times before his store in New York caught on.

English novelist John Creasey got 733 rejection slips before he published 564 books.

Babe Ruth struck out 1,330 times, but he also hit 714 home runs.

Don't worry about failure.

Worry about the chances you miss when you don't even try.

The first thing every person needs to do is face, not the possibility of failure, but the reality of failure.

Facing the Reality of Failure (4:7-9)

Paul introduces the likelihood of failure in his own life in an interesting way. He talks about the treasure we have in "earthen vessels." What does he mean? The treasure is the gospel, and the earthen vessels are our frail and fragile human bodies. God has entrusted the priceless treasure of His gospel to be kept safe in the bodies of human beings.

What happens to human bodies? They are "hard pressed . . . perplexed . . . persecuted . . . struck down" . . . but never totally defeated. Though never knocked out, we are knocked down continually in life. In other words, we fail a lot. The fact of failure is factored into our humanity. It comes with the package.

In a book titled *The Incomplete Book of Failures*, author Stephen Pile lists some of the failures associated with people you thought always did everything successfully:

- An expert said of famous football coach Vince Lombardi, "He possesses minimal football knowledge. Lacks motivation."
- Beethoven handled the violin awkwardly and preferred playing his own compositions instead of improving his technique. His teacher called him hopeless as a composer.
- Walt Disney was fired by a newspaper editor for lack of ideas. He went bankrupt several times before he built Disneyland.
- Thomas Edison's teacher said he was too stupid to learn anything.
- Albert Einstein did not speak unto he was four years old and couldn't read until he was seven. His teacher described him as "mentally slow, unsociable and adrift forever in his foolish dreams." He was expelled and refused admittance to the Zurich Polytechnic School.
- F. W. Woolworth's employers at the dry goods store where

he worked said he didn't have enough sense to wait on the customers.

- Henry Ford failed and went broke five times before he finally succeeded.
- Winston Churchill failed the sixth grade. He did not become Prime Minister of England until he was 62 and only after a lifetime of setbacks and failures.

There are many more examples which could be cited. It is true that many people who succeed significantly have a string of failures somewhere in their past.

God is not surprised by our failure. Indeed, He expects it because He knows who we are (Psalm 103:13-14). We saw in our last lesson that the disciples failed to stay awake and watch and pray with Jesus in the Garden of Gethsemane. Jesus' conclusion was, "The spirit indeed is willing, but the flesh is weak" (Matthew 26:41). God knows our propensity to fail and so understands our requests when we come to Him in times of failure (Hebrews 4:15-16).

The famous Scottish preacher, Alexander Whyte, described spiritual growth like this: "Spiritual growth is the saints falling down and getting up, falling down and getting up, falling down and getting up, all the way to heaven." If you are like me, you can identify with that!

Facing the Reason for Failure (4:17-18)

Why does God allow failure in our life? What good purpose does it serve? Verses 17 and 18 reveal four reasons for failure:

1. We fail now so that we might succeed later.

   Affliction is for now; glory is for the future. The Bible tells us that if we are going to reign with the Lord, we are going to have to suffer with Him as well (Romans 8:17). Glory is best appreciated by those who have first experienced the lack of it.

2. We fail in the incidental so that we might succeed in the important.

   Paul talks about "light affliction" and "weight of glory." The things that happen to us now, in light of eternity, are not as "heavy" as we think they are.

3. We fail in the temporary so that we might succeed in the eternal.

   Paul talks about that which is for the moment and contrasts it with that which is eternal. Our failures in time prepare us for "success" in eternity.

4. We fail outwardly so that we might succeed inwardly.

God cares far less about our outward success than He does our inward success. While we are wrapped up in what we do, God is focused on who we are. Our goal is to learn to focus on the unseen, not the seen, things—just as God does. Failure helps us do that.

Peter Marshall said, "It is better to fail in a cause that will ultimately succeed than to succeed in a cause that will ultimately fail." Though our earthen vessels may fail, the treasure we carry in them will not. We may fail on the way to heaven, but we will get there in Christ.

Facing the Result of Failure (4:16)

I love verse 16, "we do not lose heart." Why don't we lose heart? Because in spite of all the failure we experience year after year in our lives, "the inward man is being renewed day by day." On a daily basis God is transforming our inner man. We do not put our emphasis and priority on succeeding in the outward realm because that world is perishing. It is the inner man and the inward world that God is refreshing and renewing day by day.

Given these tremendous truths, the reality is that failure is not fun. It is painful and discouraging when it happens. And that's when the giant of discouragement is ready to pounce on us, to convince us to throw in the towel. How do we fight this giant when he comes 'round?

FIGHTING THE GIANT OF FAILURE
Acknowledge Your Failure

Overcoming failure—and profiting from it—begins with us. Former President Harry Truman knew how to honestly evaluate things, even his own life. When asked if he was popular as a child in school, he replied, "No. I was never popular. The popular boys were the ones who were good at games and had big fists. I was never like that. Without my glasses, I was blind as a bat, and to tell the truth, I was kind of a sissy. If there was any chance of getting into a fight, I took off. I guess that's why I'm here today." In modern language, he "failed" at being popular, but he wasn't afraid to admit it.

Sometimes we hesitate to admit our failure because we think of it like confessing sin. All sin is a failure of some sort, but not all failure is sin. So don't be afraid to admit it when you fail.

Accept God's Forgiveness

If our failure is due to sin, the only way to overcome its effects is to confess it to God and receive His forgiveness. The clear testimony of Scripture is that God is a forgiving God. He does not condone our sinful failures, but neither does He hold them against us if we want to be forgiven for them (Psalm 103:10; 1 John 1:9).

Apply the Lessons of Failure Toward Success

We should never accept failure as the final judgment or assessment of our potential. If we did that, we would never move beyond our first failure. We must learn to use failure as a resource, as an opportunity. An assistant to Thomas Edison tried to console him after a string of failed experiments had produced no results. "Oh, we have lots of results," Edison said. "We know 700 things that won't work!" John Keates, an English author, once wrote, "Failure is in a sense the highway to success, inasmuch as every discovery of what is false leads us to seek earnestly after what is true, and every fresh experience points out some form of error which we shall afterward carefully avoid."

By studying our failures we will discover what we are doing wrong which can only lead us more quickly to what to do right.

Accept Failure as a Fact of Life, Not a Way of Life

Failure is an event, not a person; failure is something that happens, not someone you become. We carelessly use the phrase, "I'm a failure," so frequently that we begin to believe it. A person can have hundreds and hundreds of failures in his life and still be a success. Or, if he allows just a few failures to overcome him, he could be on the road to characterizing himself as a failure.

Think about Peter's failure to identify with the Lord Jesus on the night of His arrest. And then think about him preaching with fire at Pentecost in the opening of the book of Acts. Peter failed, but he wasn't a failure.

Arise from Failure and Start Again

The temptation when we fail is to wallow in self-pity, to sulk, to feel sorry for ourselves (a sure sign of the influence of the giant of failure). The best thing you can do is stand up, brush yourself off, and start moving forward again.

One of my favorite characters in Scripture is Jonah. You know his story, how God told Him to go one way (east to Nineveh) and he went the other (west toward Spain). Jonah failed miserably in his role and responsibility as a prophet. Yet after he had come back to the Lord, God gave him a second chance (Jonah 3:1-2). He sent him again to Nineveh to preach and 120,000 people repented before God. It was one of the greatest responses to the Word of God recorded in history. And this from a man who just a short time previously had failed miserably.

Sometimes when you try to start over people will say, "You're a failure." That's the enemy talking—don't listen. You listen to God who wants you to succeed. If you are right with Him He will be right with you.

Avoid Judging Failure in Others

Just as others might judge us, we must be on guard against judging others as a failure. We'll close this lesson by looking at the examples of three people who were judged by others as failures, but whom God saw as successes.

1. The rich man and the beggar.

In Luke 16 the story of the rich man and Lazarus reveals two opposite individuals. Outwardly the rich man was the success and Lazarus the failure. But God's perspective was the opposite. The rich man ended up in agony, and Lazarus ended up being comforted in Paradise. If we had seen the two before knowing God's evaluation, would we have been quick to judge? God's values are often very different than ours.

2. A Pharisee and a tax collector.

In Luke 18 we have the story of a Pharisee and a tax collector. The Pharisee was the epitome of success within first-century Judaism, and the tax collector one of the most despised men in town. But when they went to the temple to pray, their true success and failure became obvious. The Pharisee was proud and arrogant, the tax collector humble and repentant. Which would we have chosen as the success and which the failure?

3. A Pharisee and a prostitute.

In Luke 7, we have the story of a Pharisee named Simon and a sinful woman, a prostitute. Simon invited Jesus to his home for dinner. A prostitute came into the dinner and anointed Jesus feet with perfume and her tears. Simon was offended because of her impropriety, but Jesus was offended at Simon's lack of love. The man who appeared to be successful was a failure when it came to love for God. The prostitute, a failure in life, succeeded in loving God. Which would we have chosen as successful and which as a failure?

These stories warn us to beware of judging others who appear to us to be failures. The man who, from the world's point of view, was a great failure turned out to be the man God exalted and honored by raising Him from the dead and seating Him at the right hand of the throne of God. Don't fall into the trap of thinking you are a failure when you fail. Defeat the giant of failure by striving to receive Jesus' final words about your life, "Well done, good and faithful servant."

APPLICATION

1. Read Matthew 26:69-27:5.
   a. What failure did Peter experience on the night of Jesus' arrest?

   b. How many times in a matter of minutes did he fail in the same way?

   c. What was his immediate response? (verse 26:75)

   d. What was Judas' failure during the same night? (verse 27:3)

   e. What was Judas' response to his failure? (verse 27:5)

   f. What does both Peter's and Judas' immediate responses tell you about the universal human response to failure?

   g. Where do we next meet up with Peter? (John 20:2 ff.)

   h. What appears to have happened to Peter's initial response to his failure?

   i. This was less than 72 hours after his failure. How would he still have been feeling on the inside?

   j. How do you reconcile Peter's inner feelings (guilt over failure) and his outward expressions of involvement and faithfulness with the other disciples?

   k. What does that tell you about picking up the pieces from failure and moving on even though we may still have conflicting feelings over our failure?

2. Describe a time in your life when you failed in a large way:
   a. What was your response? How did you handle the failure?

b. What would you have done differently?

c. Are you better prepared for your "next" failure? What is your current perspective on the place of failure in the process of spiritual maturity?

d. What insight from this lesson was most helpful to you?

3. Read Matthew 26:31-35.
   a. What was Peter's attitude toward his ability to fail? (verses 33, 35)

   b. What possibility did he see for others failing? (verse 33)

   c. What do you make of the fact that Peter was the most vocal (see verse 35b) about his not failing and the fact that he was the only one who failed (as far as we know)?

   d. How would you describe Peter's attitude at this point?

   e. What connection do you think there is between our expectations concerning failure and our response to it when it happens?

   f. While the other disciples didn't lie three times about their relationship with Jesus, how did they also fail? (compare verse 31 with verse 56b)

4. Read John 21:1-23.
   a. What did Jesus do to encourage the disciples, Peter especially, after the resurrection? (verses 2-3, 6, 11-14; 15-17).

   b. How do you think Jesus' commissioning of Peter encouraged him following his failure?

   c. Describe a time when you have been either the encourager or the "encouragee" after an experience of failure. What difference did it make?

d. How do we know that Peter indeed recovered from his failure? (Acts 2:14 ff., 3:6; 4:19; 5:29).

e. What is most important—the initial, or the long-term, response to failure?

DID YOU KNOW?

One evening when Thomas Edison came home from work, his wife told him she thought he had been working too hard, that he needed to take a vacation. "Where would I go?" Edison asked. "Just go where you would rather be than any other place in the world," she replied. "Very well," the inventor said, "I'll go tomorrow." The next morning he was back at work in his laboratory. If you are reading this lesson by the light of an electric lamp, you should be thankful that Edison's hundreds of failures didn't drive him from his lab. The inventor who patented over 1,000 inventions—including the light bulb—thrived on failure. Each failure eliminated one more rock from a field he was convinced would bear fruit in time.

FACING THE GIANT OF JEALOUSY

Selected Scriptures

---

*In this lesson we learn where to look for jealousy
and how to defeat it.*

OUTLINE

Many people think they've got jealousy under control—until it gets
out of control (and then uncontrollable). Because jealousy is so subtle,
it pays to learn where it lurks so as to be on guard. Forewarned is
forearmed when it comes to defeating this particular giant.

   I. **Jealousy Travels in Circles**
      A. Jealous Travels in Proprietary Circles
      B. Jealousy Travels in Power Circles
      C. Jealousy Travels in Performance Circles
      D. Jealousy Travels in Professional Circles
      E. Jealousy Travels in Personal Circles

  II. **The Characteristics of Jealousy**
      A. Jealousy Destroys Others
      B. Jealousy Destroys Ourselves

 III. **Facing the Giant of Jealousy**
      A. Renounce Jealousy as Sin
      B. Remember Your Rival in Prayer
      C. Reaffirm God's Goodness to You
      D. Rekindle God's Love in Your Heart

An ancient Greek legend sets the stage for our final lesson in which we confront and learn to defeat the giant of jealousy. It seems a young Greek athlete ran in a race and placed second. In honor of the winner his village erected a large statue in the town square. Envy and jealousy attacked the runner who came in second to the degree that he made plans to destroy the statue. Each night, under cover of darkness, he went out and chipped away at the foundation of the statue, expecting it to fall on its own some day. One night, however, he chipped too much. The statue's weakened base began to crack until it popped. The huge marble statue came down upon the disgruntled athlete. He died under the crushing weight of the one he had come to hate.

The truth is he died long before the statue fell on him. In giving up his heart to envy and jealousy he had ceased to live for himself. He became a slave to the giant of jealousy. His heart had become a picture of the Greek word "envy," which means "to boil within."

Shakespeare called jealousy the green sickness. To be jealous means to strike out at what somebody else is or what somebody else has. Whereas Scripture says that we are to rejoice with those who rejoice and weep with those who weep, the jealous person does the opposite. He rejoices when others weep, and weeps when others rejoice. Another's setback is his opportunity for advancement; another's sorrow his chance to gain the ascendancy. When the person of whom he is jealous is successful, he turns green with envy. When that person experiences failure, he flushes with the chance to make up lost ground.

Jealousy can eat away at one's insides as Proverbs suggests (Proverbs 14:30). No giant is more destructive to self and to relationships than the giant of jealousy and envy. To close our study without conquering this giant would leave one vulnerable. Why leave alive the one giant that can erode the peace and joy gained by conquering all of the others?

JEALOUSY TRAVELS IN CIRCLES

Jealousy makes its way through a number of networks, or circles, that we each travel in. To be aware of its favorite pathways is to be forearmed against its power.

Jealousy Travels in Proprietary Circles

Jealousy is found in the arena of possessions and wealth. For instance, Genesis 26:13-14 describes the wealth Isaac accumulated and how the Philistines "envied him." Isaac's possessions are mentioned three times so we know he had accumulated quite a lot. And though the Philistines were wealthy sea-faring traders, they still envied what Isaac had. Jealousy can easily get a foothold among the wealthy. It's easy to want just a little bit more than we already have.

To be sure, it is possible to have wealth and not envy what anyone else has. God has blessed many Christians with significant wealth and many of them have learned to live with gratitude toward God instead of envy toward others. But generally speaking, jealousy and envy have an easy time stirring up trouble in the circles of the wealthy.

Jealousy Travels in Power Circles

Not only does wealth envy wealth, but power envies power. Miriam and Aaron were jealous of Moses' power and position among the people (Numbers 12:1 ff.), as was Korah (Numbers 16:1 ff.). In the books of Kings and Chronicles we read story after story of kings who usurped the power of other kings, often by criminal and traitorous acts, only to have the same thing happen to them once they reached the pinnacle of power. History is littered with the ruins of nations whose leaders, motivated by jealousy and envy, led them to war.

In the four gospels and the book of Acts we read where the Jewish leaders were jealous of Jesus' power and influence among the people, and later that of His apostles. They crucified Jesus and threw His apostles into jail—and worse (Acts 7:54-8:1)—in part on the basis of jealousy and fear that their own power-base was eroding.

Power circles can be a breeding ground for jealousy in the business world—and even in the church. Whose organization is biggest? Who's getting the most media attention? Who has the most employees? Power can promote jealousy among those who have it.

Jealousy Travels in Performance Circles

If there is a circle where Christians are most vulnerable, this is probably it—individually and corporately. Remember the story in the Old Testament of Saul and David? David became the young hero in Israel after he slew the Philistine giant, Goliath. The green sickness of jealousy began to grow in Saul's heart as he saw the hearts of Israel go out to David. Saul spent the rest of his life trying to eliminate the object of his jealousy, tracking David all over the Judean wilderness trying to kill him. He remained a captive to his jealousy until he died.

The local church, I am ashamed to say, is a place where jealousy lurks, waiting for a chance to attack. Perhaps it is because the church is a "volunteer" organization. People give their money and "volunteer" their time and, as a result, feel they are entitled to certain things—sing a solo, chair a committee, receive recognition when those roles, responsibilities, and recognition are given to others. How subtle and insidious the enemy is to stir up jealousy and envy in our midst, and how naïve we are to succumb to it!

Every Christian needs to remind himself that we who are saved by the grace and mercy of God have given up all our personal rights. For us to think we deserve something that Christ has given to another is to contradict the love we say we have for Him. The church of Jesus Christ is the last place the giant of jealousy should ever find a home.

Jealousy Travels in Professional Circles

An amazing example of envy occurred once when Paul was incarcerated for preaching the gospel. While he was in jail, others were taking advantage of his imprisonment and preaching the gospel hoping to gain for themselves some of the attention Paul had received (Philippians 1:15-16). And Paul had an interesting response. He said that even though others were preaching the gospel using envy as a motive (some were also preaching from proper motives), he took comfort knowing that the gospel was being proclaimed. He didn't respond angrily or out of resentment which would have revealed jealousy in his own life—that others were gathering to themselves "fame" which was rightly his. He was content to sit in his jail cell and allow God to sort out the motives in men's hearts. He was simply happy that the gospel was being preached.

Jealousy Travels in Personal Circles

We may not be wealthy or powerful, have roles to perform or other professionals to compete with—but we are all people. And unfortunately, jealousy shows up most often in the relationships we have with other people just like ourselves. This is probably where we see it the most and certainly where we see it the most in the Bible. In the Old Testament, Cain was jealous of Abel, Ishmael was jealous of Isaac, and Jacob and Esau were jealous of each other. And Joseph's brothers were so envious of him that they sold him into slavery. In the New Testament, the prodigal son story gives us a sad illustration of jealousy (Luke 15:11-32). We are often so involved in focusing on the prodigal and his return to the father that we miss the burning jealousy of the older brother. He was incensed that his father had never rewarded him for his faithfulness and obedience, and here the prodigal was being welcomed home like a hero. His jealousy had blinded his eyes to his own Pharisee-like misunderstanding of love and grace.

When jealousy comes in the front door, love goes out the back door. The two cannot coexist in the same person. Rest assured that if you are struggling with jealousy you are also struggling with love.

Before looking at the characteristics of jealousy, it is important to remember that jealousy will most likely raise its head in the circles in which one travels. As a pastor and preacher, I am not jealous of athletes, plumbers, bank presidents, or shop owners, as much as I admire and respect what they do. My temptations with jealousy are going to arise in the circles in which I travel, and they will most often for you as well.

This old fable well illustrates my point: The devil was crossing the Libyan desert when he came across a group of junior devils who were tempting a holy man. They tried to tempt him with the flesh, with doubts, with fear, with lies—nothing they did could induce the holy man to sin. The devil asked the juniors to step aside so that he might show them how to reach the old man. The devil leaned forward and whispered in the man's ear, "Have you heard the news? Your brother has just been made Bishop of Alexandria." With that, a cloud of jealousy clouded the now-not-so-holy man's face—and the devil had him.

Be careful about becoming jealous in the circles in which you travel.

THE CHARACTERISTICS OF JEALOUSY

Above all else, jealousy always does two things:

Jealousy Destroys Others

Cain killed Abel. Saul tried to kill David. Herod killed babies so King Jesus wouldn't come to power in his realm. Envy and jealousy lead people to do unthinkable things to others. I recall reading a story a few years ago about a mother who killed a teenaged girl who was competing for a cheerleading spot that the woman wanted her daughter to win. Killing a child over jealousy regarding a cheerleading position!

But lest we presume ourselves immune from such acts, we need only remember the jealous thoughts we ourselves have had. Acts of jealousy begin with thoughts of jealousy.

Jealousy Destroys Ourselves

Remember in the book of Esther how Haman was hanged on the scaffold he had built for the object of his jealousy? And how those who threw Daniel in the lions den were the ones consumed? And how Joseph's brothers ended up begging for food from the object of their jealousy? And how Saul was consumed by his jealousy while David content with his psalms? The jealous person is the one who ultimately suffers the most.

There is little argument that jealousy and envy are destructive attitudes. The question is, How do we conquer them?

FACING THE GIANT OF JEALOUSY

Like many of the other giants we have covered in our study, jealousy falls into the category of personal choice. If we are jealous, it's not because we were born with it or caught it like a cold. Therefore, our strategy for conquering jealousy is based on what it is: a sinful choice we make.

Renounce Jealousy as Sin

We read in the gospels that Jesus Christ was handed over and put to death because of envy (Matthew 27:18; Mark 15:10). Every time I begin to get comfortable accommodating jealousy and envy in my life I need to remember how sinful they are—sinful enough to have caused the death of the sinless Son of God. If those responsible for the death of Christ did so on the basis of sinful envy, why is my envy any less sinful than theirs? It is not. Envy and jealousy are the same in every human heart—sinful choices that we choose to indulge in and nurture.

First and foremost, jealousy must be renounced as sin.

Remember Your Rival in Prayer

If you are jealous of another person, the best thing to do is pray for that person and thank God for their success or good fortune or whatever it is you envy. A story is told about two famous preachers in London. F. B. Meyer was the older, established preacher and Charles Spurgeon was the younger, newer preacher in town. When Spurgeon became the toast of the town—he preached to tens of thousands on Sunday and the newspaper printed his sermons on the front page—Meyer began to envy him. But he immediately began to pray for his success. Soon, because of his partnership in prayer, Meyer was able to rejoice in the blessings of God upon Spurgeon. And his own church eventually benefited greatly from the upsurge in spiritual interest in London.

Pray for those for whom you feel the slightest twinge of envy.

Reaffirm God's Goodness to You

Here is something important I have learned about jealousy: It is almost always because we don't think God has been as good to us as we think He should have been. If we are jealous of another person, it is because we want the blessings God has given to him. We don't understand why He has blessed them and not us, and we become jealous of what they have that we don't have. The quickest way to put an end to that kind of thinking is to take an inventory of our own blessings.

If we have anything at all it is because we have been blessed. All we deserve is judgment. But all of us have far more than we deserve, and most of us have far more than we need. When we begin to thank God for all that He has blessed us with—stop right now and consider your blessings!—it will be hard to continue in a jealous frame of mind toward another. In the purposes of God, how could we possibly be jealous of what He has done for another when He has done so much for us? Thanksgiving will douse the spark of jealousy and fan the flames of gratitude every time.

Rekindle God's Love in Your Heart

First Corinthians 13:4 holds the key to defeating the giant of jealousy: "Love does not envy." Where love is, envy cannot abide. If envy marches in the front door, love will sweep it out the back door. If jealousy sneaks in the back, love will usher it out the front. The house of love has no room for jealousy to even visit, much less take up residence.

Rekindle God's love by reading the Word and through prayer. Ask God to fill you with His Spirit whose fruit is love. Then act on those prayers by manifesting the love of God to any person toward whom you have felt envy or jealousy. Your walk must match your talk when it comes to love triumphing over jealousy.

My prayer for you as we conclude our study of spiritual giants is that Jesus Christ will be the only spiritual giant in your life. Where He is Lord and King there can be no fear, discouragement, loneliness, worry, guilt, temptation, anger, resentment, doubt, procrastination, permanent failure, or jealousy. Abide in Him, and let His Word abide in you, and you will walk in victory over every would-be giant you encounter.

1. Record your insights on envy from the following verses in Proverbs:
   a. 3:31

   b. 6:34

   c. 14:30

   d. 23:17

   e. 24:1

   f. 24:19

   g. 27:4

2. Read 2 Corinthians 11:1-4.
   a. How does Paul introduce his discussion so his readers know he is engaging in a play on words? (verse 1)

   b. How can jealousy be "godly?" (verse 2)

   c. What is the situation which caused Paul to be "jealous" for the believers in Corinth? (verses 2-4)

   d. How "jealous" does Paul appear to be in attempting to rescue the Corinthians from their apostolic "suitors?" (see the remainder of chapters 11 and 12)

   e. Paul says that God is provoking Israel to jealousy by giving the blessings of the covenant to the Gentiles (Romans 10:19; 11:11). Since jealousy can have both a positive and a negative aspect, how do we tell whether our jealousy is sinful or not?

   f. Have you ever experienced a godly kind of jealousy for a person or a cause?

   g. What efforts did you make to "rescue" the object of your jealousy?

h. How were your efforts received?

i. What convinced you that your jealousy was legitimate?

3. With what does Paul lump envy in 1 Corinthians 3:3?

a. How does he characterize those who practice sinful envy?

b. How serious a sin does Paul make envy out to be in Galatians 5:19-21?

c. What kind of a "work" is envy? (Galatians 5:19)

d. Therefore, of whom is envy characteristic?

e. What are the characteristics in this list compared in Galatians 5:22-23?

f. Who produces the characteristics in this second list?

g. If a Christian engages in envy or jealousy, what might we say he is doing? (Ephesians 4:30; 1 Thessalonians 5:19)

h. If a Christian is envious or jealous, what can we be sure he is NOT doing? (Galatians 5:25-26)

4. In what circles are you most likely to be tempted with envy or jealousy?

DID YOU KNOW?

There is a thin line between being "zealous" and being "jealous." The former we think of as a positive thing, the latter as a negative. In truth, they both have roots in the same idea. The Greek work *zelos* (which may have derived from the verb *zeo*, to boil or be hot) meant fury or warmth or zeal. In other words, both the zealous and the jealous have a passion for the object of their *zelos*. A zealot could be passionate about a good thing or an evil thing; a jealous person could be jealous for godly or carnal reasons.

Turning Point
Resources
By Dr. David Jeremiah

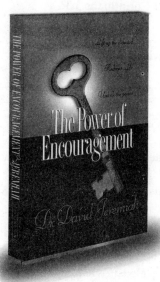

The Power of Encouragement
by Dr. David Jeremiah

In this volume, Dr. Jeremiah examines the heart of self-giving, genuine love – and suggests helpful ways to learn to express the kind of encouragement that heals, unites, and renews our zest for life.

Scriptural and uplifting, *The Power of Encouragement* has the potential to radically reshape the world and equip people as ambassadors of the God of Love.

POEBK (Soft Cover Book) . . $13
POESG (Study Guide) . . $9
POEAL (Cassette Album) . . $50

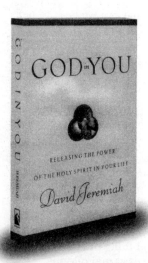

God in You
Many Christians find the Holy Spirit the hardest person of the Holy Trinity to understand. Leaving abstract concepts behind, this book reveals God's Spirit in concrete terms. It brings a fresh, clear image of how the Holy Spirit affects our everyday lives as God is in us and with us.

GIYHBK (Hardback) $19
GIYSG 1, 2 (Study Guides, 2 volumes) $18
GIYAL (Cassette Albums, 2 volumes) $75

ORDER 1-800-947-1993

Turning Point
Resources
By Dr. David Jeremiah

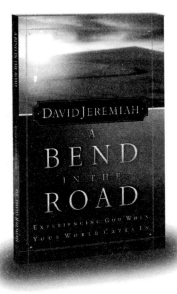

A Bend in the Road
This new book offers inspiring real-life stories of people who have struggled with terminal illness, the loss of a child, the imprisonment of a spouse, and other disruptive moments. Dr. Jeremiah interweaves his own journal entries, revealing his battle with cancer and how the Psalms helped to sustain him during the fight of his life.

A Bend in the Road is an invaluable source of help and encouragement for people facing major obstacles in life.

BIR-HBK (Hard Cover Book) $19
BIR-SG (Study Guide) $9
BIR-AL (Cassette Album, 11 tapes) $55

Prayer—The Great Adventure
Dr. David Jeremiah explores "The Lord's Prayer," which Jesus gave to His disciples, and explains how you can put that pattern into practice in your own life. As you study this prayer and begin to implement our Lord's teaching, you'll become more thankful for what He has done and begin to see His power at work.

PGA-HBK (Hard Cover Book) $19
PGA-SG (Study Guide) $9

OTHER STUDY GUIDES & BOOKS

A complete catalog of resources is available from Turning Point, call 1-800-947-1993. An audiocassette album is available for each series. See the catalog for additional series.

SELECTION	CODE	QTY	PRICE	TOTAL

STUDY GUIDES

SELECTION	CODE	QTY	PRICE	TOTAL
Bend in the Road, A (Comfort)	BIRSG	_____	$ 9	$ _____
Christians Have Stress Too	CHSSG	_____	$ 9	_____
Core Values of the Church (1 Corinthians, 3 volumes)	CVCSG1,2,3	_____	$ 27	_____
Escape the Coming Night (Revelation, 4 volumes)	REVSG1,2,3,4	_____	$ 36	_____
Fruit of the Spirit, The (Galatians 5:16-26)	FOSSG	_____	$ 9	_____
Gifts from God	GFGSG	_____	$ 9	_____
God in You (Holy Spirit, 2 volumes)	GIYSG1,2	_____	$ 18	_____
God Meant It for Good (Life of Joseph, 2 volumes)	JOSSG1,2	_____	$ 18	_____
Greatest Stories Ever Told, The (Parables)	GSTSG	_____	$ 9	_____
Handwriting on the Wall, The (Daniel, 3 volumes)	HOWSG1,2,3	_____	$ 27	_____
Home Improvement	HMISG	_____	$ 9	_____
How to Live According to Jesus (2 volumes)	HTLSG1,2	_____	$ 18	_____
Invasion of Other Gods (New Age)	IOGSG	_____	$ 9	_____
Issues of the Home and Family	IHFSG	_____	$ 9	_____
Jesus' Final Warning (Prophecy)	JFWSG	_____	$ 9	_____
Knowing the God You Worship	KGWSG	_____	$ 9	_____
Life of David: The Tender Warrior, The (2 volumes)	TTWSG1,2	_____	$ 18	_____
Living by Faith (Romans, 3 volumes)	ROMSG	_____	$ 27	_____
Nation in Crisis, A (Joshua, 2 Volumes)	NICSG1,2	_____	$ 18	_____
Overcoming Loneliness	OCLSG	_____	$ 9	_____
People Who Met Jesus	PMJSG	_____	$ 9	_____
Power of Encouragement, The	POESG	_____	$ 9	_____
Power of Love, The (1 Corinthians 13)	POLSG	_____	$ 9	_____
Prayer–The Great Adventure	PGASG	_____	$ 9	_____
Runaway Prophet–Jonah, The	TRPSG	_____	$ 9	_____
Ruth, Romance & Redemption	RRRSG	_____	$ 9	_____
Signs of the Second Coming (Matthew 24 & 25)	SSCSG	_____	$ 9	_____
Spiritual Warfare (Ephesians 6)	SPWSG	_____	$ 9	_____
Stewardship Is Lordship	SIL	_____	$ 9	_____
Turning Toward Integrity (James)	TTISG	_____	$ 9	_____
Turning Toward Joy (Philippians)	TTJSG	_____	$ 9	_____
What the Bible Says About Angels	ANGSG	_____	$ 9	_____
When Wisdom Turns to Foolishness (Solomon)	WTFSG	_____	$ 9	_____
Worship	WORSG	_____	$ 9	_____

BOOKS

SELECTION	CODE	QTY	PRICE	TOTAL
Bend in the Road, A	BIRHBK	_____	$ 19	_____
Escape the Coming Night (Revelation)	REVBK	_____	$ 13	_____
Gifts from God (Parenting)	GFGHBK	_____	$ 19	_____
God in You (The Holy Spirit)	GIYHBK	_____	$ 19	_____
Handwriting on the Wall, The (Daniel)	HOWBK	_____	$ 12	_____
Invasion of Other Gods (New Age)	IOGBK	_____	$ 13	_____
Jesus' Final Warning (Prophecy)	JFWHBK	_____	$ 19	_____
Power of Encouragement, The	POEBK	_____	$ 13	_____
Prayer–The Great Adventure	PGAHBK	_____	$ 19	_____
What the Bible Says About Angels	ANGHBK	_____	$ 19	_____

To order by Discover, Visa, or MasterCard call:

1-800-947-1993

POSTAGE AND HANDLING CHART

For orders	Add
Up to $5.99	$1.50
$6.00-$19.99	$2.50
$20.00-$50.99	$3.50
$51.00-$99.99	$6.00
$100.00 & over	$9.00

MERCHANDISE TOTAL	_____
SHIPPING/HANDLING	_____
SUBTOTAL	_____
CA RESIDENTS ONLY	
ADD 7.25% TAX	_____
GIFT TO MINISTRY	_____
TOTAL	$ _____

Please enclose payment with order. Make check or money order payable to:

TURNING POINT • P.O. Box 3838 • San Diego, CA 92163-1838 *(Please allow 4-6 weeks for delivery.)*

Mr./Mrs./Miss _____

Address _____

City/State/Zip _____

I listen to *Turning Point* on (station call letters): _____ Phone _____